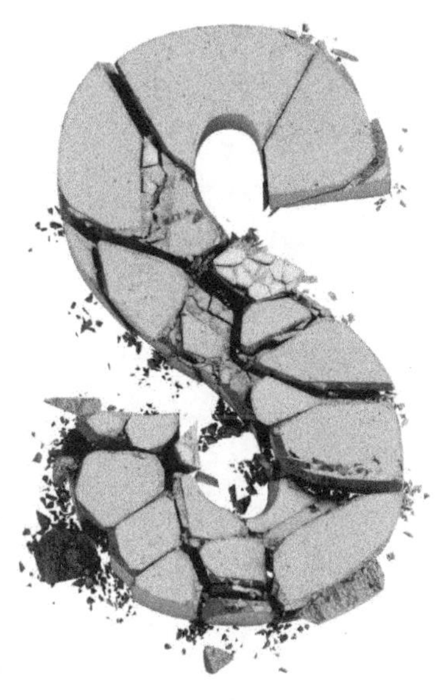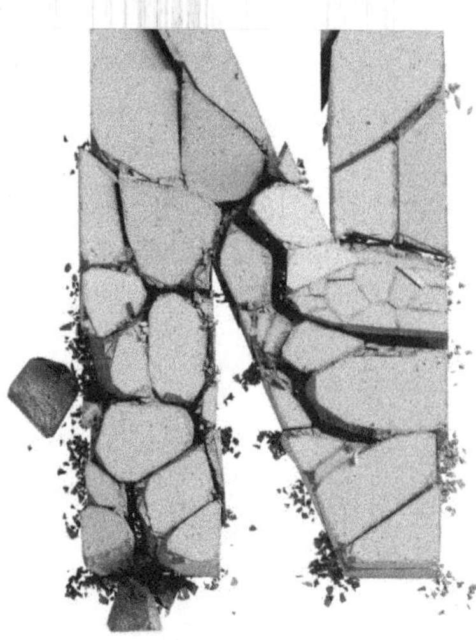

WHAT IT IS, HOW IT AFFECTS YOU AND HOW IT CAN BE OVERCOME.

David Ross Sherman

Interior Design by The Book Bureau

Printed in the United States of America.
ISBN: 978-1-960548-49-8 (paperback)
       978-1-960548-50-4 (ebook)

The Book Bureau

CONTENTS

All scripture references are from The New King James Version of the Holy Bible unless otherwise noted

SIN

PREFACE

2 Chronicles 7:14

if My people who are called by My name will humble themselves, and pray and seek My face, and turn from their wicked ways, then I will hear from heaven, and will forgive their sin and heal their land.

I am truly amazed that in my research I was not able to find a book entitled SIN. There are, of course, many books regarding sin and many covering subjects found in this book. Hopefully, this condensation of subjects relating to sin will be able to touch your soul in order that you may be able to go forth in your life and sin no more.

Being forgiven from sin may not seem like a big deal to some people, but it is. Sin keeps us from having a relationship with God, the most powerful, majestic, loving and compassionate being in the universe. And who wouldn't want that? Well, apparently anyone who doesn't believe that such a being exists. If He doesn't exist, then you have no worries. But if He does and He is all the things I just described, then perhaps you would desire to investigate. Speaking from personal experience, I can state unequivocally that He does exist. I have experienced miracles and seen things that convince me that I am living in truth.

In the verse above we see a formula. God is big on formulas. We see them throughout the bible. But this one is the formula for forgiveness of your sin which are the offenses that have kept you from Him for so long. We see that the author (God) is speaking to those who are called by His name; His children, His heirs. They are proud, because they are children of the king but must become humble, because that is what He is. They must be in prayer, which is communication with Him and they must seek His face, which means to seek knowledge of Him as well as a relationship with Him and they must repent from their sin. That basically means they must stop doing it. And that, my friend, is the hard part. But the rewards are sure and they are immeasurable. Forgiven sin and a healed land are the promise. On an personal level that translates to forgiven sin and a healed soul. That is worth it by any measure. But sin is so attractive. It feels good. It gives you sensations like nothing else.

Imagine yourself floating in a magnificent, but tiny bay in a tropical paradise on a floating mat or tube. It is peaceful. The walls of the surrounding canyon offer protection from the world as well as a cooling shade as you float in the tepid water. Your mind is focused on the One who has brought you to this wonderful place and you are sustained by this same presence. He is providing all your needs. Life is good. It is very pleasant.

Suddenly you are bumped by something from beneath the water. It didn't hurt and as a matter of fact it gave you a kind of nice sensation. It can't be explained really, in words, but it was enough to pique your interest and pursue whatever it was. So you turn over and dive into the crystal clear water in an attempt to see whatever it was. You see an image glowing not far from you and it is inviting you to follow. Is this the being who brushed against you? It is very pleasant to look at but would be even more pleasant to hold or perhaps just touch, so you swim hard toward it. It dives down deeper as you follow and you can touch it for just a moment and that sensation returns and spurs you on to follow harder. Just when you are about to grasp this wonderful creature you remember that you are underwater and you are now in immediate need of oxygen to survive. But it is nowhere to be found. You will succumb to the desire of your flesh. You will die pursuing that thing which gave you an amazing sensation, a wonderful feeling.

This is sin. Tempting first with but a nudge, but then
inviting you to try some more. It will feel good and it will satisfy if only for a moment. Sin is something that can affect your life for what may seem like good, for how could anything that makes us feel this good be wrong? And it matters not if that sin is any of the things found in

 Galatians 5:19-21
 19 Now the works of the flesh are evident, which are: adultery, fornication, uncleanness, lewdness,
 20 idolatry, sorcery, hatred, contentions, jealousies, outbursts of wrath, selfish ambitions, dissensions, heresies,

That's not even a comprehensive list of sin, for it doesn't mention stealing or lying or even covetousness. (I'm pretty sure all of those are sin too) but it does give us an idea of the mindset of those who sin. Selfish ambitions are such things. To have selfish ambitions it means you are centered on yourself. This may seem abstract to some but it is quite true that if you are centered on yourself you will not be able to love God or your neighbor, which are the two things Jesus said that if we accomplish, will automatically enable us to keep all the commandments of God.

So you can see why selfish ambitions could be detrimental in a relationship with God. But sin does not cause a relationship problem with only God, sin will cause problems in every relationship you have. Since we've already established that sin is always self-centered, it can't help but affect our other relationships as well. All good relationships are based on giving, or at least they should be. People who are self centered cannot have healthy relationships with other people. They don't care about others, so how could they? Oh, they may seem to care for a bit, but if they are truly in love with themselves, then that caring will show up sporadically and then with less frequency and finally disappear altogether.

Sin affects our lives in so many ways we cannot begin to fathom all of it until we begin to take it seriously. When we do that, we will most certainly discover that we have entered into a state of warfare. And it won't be pretty. Warfare is never pretty. And this war has two fronts; A physical front as well as a spiritual front. It will involve death and destruction. It will be painful. But in the end, when you are standing victorious over the thing that has haunted you, chased you, controlled you and defeated you so many times, you will feel a sense of victory and accomplishment you will find nowhere else. Spiritual victories are the best because they are everlasting. They bring you closer to God in ways you can't imagine and once you accomplish this you can do as Jesus told the woman taken in adultery…"Go and sin no more".

I wrote this book because sin has overtaken the lives of many people, even Christians who may have a secret sin of which no one knows. And it seems as though sin has taken over the heart of America. God's judgments are not only held out for the individual, but for nations. But to turn the heart of a nation, it must be done one person at a time. You may know someone who is involved in a sin that is deeply troubling and you may not even be aware. We must not angrily confront those involved in any sin, but rather show them the love of Jesus. To convert a sinner, you would do well to show them a path that will offer them peace through love so they will willingly leave their sin behind.

But it is possible that you, yourself are involved in a secret sin which you have been unable to conquer. It keeps returning again and again and you are tired of it. Believe me, you can defeat it, but only with the formula God has provided in His word.

Turn the page to begin your journey to victory.

CHAPTER ONE

What is sin?

Ephesians 6:12

For we do not wrestle against flesh and blood, but against principalities, against powers, against the rulers of the darkness of this age, against spiritual hosts of wickedness in the heavenly places

I am certainly not going to list all the sins that mankind is able to commit, for that would be a book in itself. Sin is many things. But most of all it is an absence of love. We were created for love. That's why Jesus said that all of the law and all of the prophets could be contained in, "Love God with all your heart and soul and mind and love your neighbor as yourself." (Matthew 22:37-39) That's how we do not sin. Instead we love. It's all about love. Who knew? Well, we all should have known. In Exodus, chapter 20, God lays out the Ten Commandments. From these ten laws we can see that it is hard to convince someone you love them if you are lying to them or about them or stealing from them or either having with them or hiding adultery from them. You get my point. There isn't much love in sin. According to 1John 4:8 God is love so it stands to reason that any creation he has made has love built into it... somewhere. In some though, it is very difficult to find. It exists in the nature of every single breathing creation of God. Animals even love one another. Sometimes love is even found between different species. I love my dogs. Sin keeps us from love.

So it's no wonder that God does not like sin.

I said in my first book, "Learning to Agalliao" that we will one day all realize that we are spiritual beings having a physical experience, not physical beings occasionally having a spiritual experience. This is what Paul was trying to tell us in Ephesians 6:12 at the beginning of this chapter. If you do not understand this concept, this book will be of absolutely no use to you. Sorry, no refunds. But I do suggest that you stop and consider the depth and understanding of your own spirituality before reading farther by reading and then contemplating that verse before continuing.

Welcome back. Now that you have taken a moment to think about how you take charge of your actions and your thoughts, understand this; You are involved in a war and much of the problem with what is happening in our world today is that no one seems to understand that they are standing in the middle of a battlefield. Souls are dying eternal death each day because they failed to realize one simple truth: We are spiritual beings. If we don't even understand who we really are, how can we possibly overcome principalities, which means a chief, a boss or a commander or against powers and rulers over darkness of this age or against spiritual hosts of wickedness that exist in a place we can't even see? We must get in touch with our spirituality. It is imperative if we are to be not only successful, but triumphant against some very powerful enemies. These enemies, I'll call them what they are; demons, spawn of hell, disgusting venomous beings whose only wish for you is to suffer like they are and that is simply because they know they will for eternity.

Does that strike a little fear into you? It should. Hell is not a place where all the "fun" people will be. There won't be much fun there. Not one single person in the bible who has ever spoken of hell has anything good to say about it. So what puts us in that position of having to be stuck in hell for eternity rather than living eternally in peace while being adorned with love?

Short answer is Jesus. You must have a relationship with Jesus. Not just walk an aisle one time and then have the expectation that you now will get your ticket punched and ride the train to glory. When He said in John 14:6 that He was the way, the truth and the life, He meant it. He is the way we understand truth and should live that truth in our lives.

Our basic nature has been corrupted, more on that in a moment, but because of that corruption, we have a tendency, perhaps even a need to break the rules. It's in our DNA. We get a thrill, howbeit a small thrill, when we do something we shouldn't. And we somehow, innately know for the most part what we should and should not do.

We start young

Try to remember when you were a small child and you were in the grocery store and perhaps you saw some candy and you put it in your pocket. It was just laying there. So you picked it up and put it in your pocket for later. When you got home and you decided to have that candy, you slipped it out of your coat pocket and opened it. Mom came into the room and immediately confronted you about how you acquired this candy. You honestly told her you took it from the store. She tells you that what you did was stealing and it is wrong. We must pay for what we use in this life. You are confused. It was just laying there. To you, there was nothing wrong. Or was there? Now you know what you must do. You must *hide* it when you want something that mommy doesn't want you to have. You are forming a pattern of sin without even knowing it. If not controlled it could escalate into many ways to steal from others.

Or perhaps you were a young child and something touched your genitals and sparked an interest in that area of your body. You found that with touch came a wonderful feeling that was very exciting and very difficult to repress. No one ever explained to you that it was wrong, but even if they did, you may not stop the action, but rather just become creative in ways to hide it. A pattern of sin is being formed. If left uncontrolled, a predatory psychopathic murderer could be on the loose. Of course, that is taking the scenario to its worst resolution, but the potential is still there.

Let's explore still another scenario. You did something you knew was wrong but no one knew it was you who did it. There were no witnesses, so when confronted about it and questioned by mom or dad, you simply lied and said you didn't do it. You were believed. So, now you will continue this behavior to get what you want when you want it. You are honing the skills to become a successful liar. You may desire to lie about other things, things that do not matter, but your skill at lying is impressive, so you exaggerate everything. You find you cannot cease from stretching the truth about everything. You have become a compulsive liar.

How did it get here?

We all should know how sin entered into this world and forever changed how we interact with God. Adam and Eve simply took a bite of something God had forbidden them to eat. Some believe this story may be a metaphor for something else but we have no evidence of that so I will continue under that premise. With this in mind I would say the most basic of answers to the question of "what is sin?" is simply disobedience to God.

Now, why would God care about what fruit you were eating? Well this particular fruit was what would give them knowledge of good and evil. Before, they only knew good, and now evil would be known to them and it will have a very serious consequence in their lives. You see, the sin wasn't eating the fruit, it was eating the fruit that God said not to eat. Disobedience has consequences. Now some would say, "Why does God get to make the rules?". Well, short answer; He is God. His ways are higher than our ways, His thoughts higher than our thoughts. He is the creator and we are the creation. (Isaiah 55) And because He is the creator and He has our best interests in mind, He knows what will be best for us, each of us. He is attempting to guide us into safety. It's no different than someone telling a small child not to wander out onto the street. You may yell loudly at the child and even spank him to get him to understand the seriousness of the situation. He will cry. It has caused him though, to consider the seriousness of the situation. Death could result from the child being run over by a car. He won't do that again…probably.

> *Gen 3:6*
> *So when the woman saw that the tree was good for food, that it was pleasant to the eyes, and a tree desirable to make one wise, she took of its fruit and ate. She also gave to her husband with her, and he ate.*

Death did result in Adam and Eve's sin. They were created to live forever, knowing only good, communing with God, but that desire in her heart to know more, to satisfy her flesh, led Eve to take a bite of that forbidden fruit and then both sell the idea to and then pass it along to her husband. After enjoying their experience, they immediately understood wrong and evil. They immediately understood what it was to disobey God, the One who had created them. They felt guilt. They hid themselves because they were naked and they had this feeling now that something was wrong. It wasn't before but suddenly it is. They had experienced disobedience to the One who had given them life and they were confused and afraid which is always what we feel when we are guilty.

Sin brings fear

When we happen to sin, once we become aware of sin, no matter how tiny an infraction it may be, we will have a twinge of first guilt and then fear. It may be quick, a millisecond, but it will be there. That's because in our subconscious mind (our spirit) we know that we have done something wrong and we instinctively fear punishment. This is a very brief explanation of what happens but it *is* what happens. Someone may become so conditioned to sin that each time they commit the same sin the fear is lessened as well as the guilt because the person has not yet experienced the perceived punishment. A pattern of sin is formed because the punishment was not realized.

Had the person listened to the voice of fear the first time or even the second, perhaps the pattern would never have been formed and the person would be free from the control of that particular sin. But we are not creatures who learn easily. For someone to see sin in their life, they must first believe in a God whom they have offended. If someone doesn't believe in God, then they most certainly won't be able to see sin at least in their own lives. And even if they do, they won't care. Sin is only sin to those who feel guilt or fear or both at its presence. This could come from an early childhood Christian experience or simply good moral upbringing, or not. It is not requisite that one have a good childhood filled with good experiences to be able to find God or to realize a sensation of guilt after sinning. That's because love is built into our most base instincts. Even serial killers had mothers who loved them and whom they loved at one point in their lives. The sin that somehow found them slowly wore away their love and replaced it with a desire that does not involve love, but only their pleasure, and that desire can certainly run great in those who may feed it and nourish it through repeated use of fulfillment of that desire. However, to discover sin in one's self, to come to the knowledge of one's own sin, there must be some moral compunction, some feeling of doing wrong, which is what we call guilt.

Attitude is everything

The first mention of the word sin in the bible is in Gen 4:7. It is God addressing Cain which tells us that God did not cease communication with mankind after the fall of Adam and Eve. Cain was well aware of the punishment for disobedience to God because he was someone who worked a field every day to get things to grow from the ground so he could eat. This was the result of his father's sin and I'm pretty sure he didn't like it. God had just shown disrespect to Cain's offering, but respect to his brother Abel's offering. Cain became very angry at that and it was obvious to everyone. So God took him aside and said,

"If you do well, will you not be accepted? And if you do not do well, sin lies at the door. And its desire is for you, but you should rule over it."

This was about attitude. The word interpreted "do well" is yatab (yaw-tab') in Hebrew and it is a primitive root which means to be or to make well, literally (sound, beautiful) or figuratively (happy, successful, right): These are things that show a good attitude. God was warning Cain that sin has a price. It has a power all its own and it desires to own you. We know sin has power because how could something that has no power have desire and how could something that has no power rule over you? But it is conquerable, otherwise God would not have told him he should rule over it.

In fact, sin is so powerful and its control over us so strong that in the very next verse Cain killed his brother. He let his anger and jealousy fester and rise up within him until he could control it no more, completely ignoring the counsel of God, and he killed his own little brother. He succumbed to the power of the sin that was using his anger to get him worked up enough to come up behind his brother and kill him. So much for ruling over it.

Sin has power

So, we find that sin has a lot of power. And we must overcome that power if we are not to be overcome by it. I don't want to kill my brother, no matter how mean he may have been to me in my youth. Have I ever been angry with him? Well my brother once chased me down our street with a hatchet screaming, "I'll kill you!". I was about ten and he a year older. Of course I had locked him down the basement for a couple of hours, and he had to chop the door down with that hatchet to get out, so maybe it was justified. I'm glad God made me faster though. Things are good with us now, thank God. My point, though, is that sin has power of its own and the demon that has watched you grow your entire life knows all your strengths and weaknesses and waits for the appropriate time to tempt you, (when you are at your weakest) to make things happen that will frustrate you, and do innumerable things to complicate your life. What are we to do? Well thank God He took care of the problem so that we could obtain righteousness by absolving us from all guilt if we are found in Jesus Christ.

One of most difficult things to understand is that sin is sin. Even the smallest sin separates us from God…certainly not completely, for the door is always open to those who seek forgiveness through Jesus Christ. But when most of us begin in sin, we don't understand that concept of offending God simply because we don't know who God is. It is usually not until adulthood that we are able to understand what it means to really have a relationship with Him. We may, as I did, have a seeking while we are young and in their youth have a magnificent relationship with the Lord. Some people never leave that relationship from their youth, but most, I think, do leave the relationship with God they had in their youth to experience life in the world. I know I did and I now regret the 20 year hiatus I took to explore the world. I am happy I survived it, for I know many who did not and are probably suffering as we speak.

God does not look at sin the same way we do. He is able to forgive the murderer and sex offender as easily as the thief and the liar or the one disrespectful to their parents. Sin is sin to Him. It's all darkness. There are no innocent little white lies. They are all black. All sin is darkness. And the reason He hates it so very much is simply because it separates us from Him. We cannot be in a partnership or a conversation or any type of relationship with God while we are clothed in sin. The blackness of our sin covers who we are in God. Not to Him, but to us. God still is aware of our presence, but our voice is quieted by the volume of our sin. Until we come through Jesus and seek forgiveness. Peter has an interesting perspective on this in:

> *1 Peter 4:1-2*
> *1 Therefore, since Christ suffered for us in the flesh, arm yourselves also*

with the same mind, for he who has suffered in the flesh has ceased from sin,

2 that he no longer should live the rest of his time in the flesh for the lusts of men, but for the will of God.

Peter says that suffering makes us cease from sin, but we can arm ourselves and protect ourselves from sin by seeking to have the same mind of Christ in suffering. We can use the suffering of Christ to keep us from sin. But we first must understand how to do that. We will explore that in later chapters, but I wanted to put that idea in your mind. It is the entry way into holiness.

Just understand that suffering is not merely physical pain. It can be mental, emotional, physical or spiritual. When we suffer in any of these areas we seek relief. Jesus said to seek Him in your suffering and He will take your burden. But there are some hurdles.

A different world

I said at the beginning of this chapter that we must understand that we are spirits. Spiritual beings have a different outlook. Walking in the Spirit or spiritual world is different than walking in uptown Manhattan. Imagine being transported to a place where you didn't know the language, the culture, the food or anything else. No one could understand what you wanted or what you were saying and you couldn't understand anyone or any of their rules. Do you think it would be frustrating? I would be ripping my hair out in an hour. But this is precisely why we must

Be diligent to present yourself approved to God, a worker who does not need to be ashamed, rightly dividing the word of truth. 2 Tim 2:15

This is why studying the bible is so very important. It would be impossible to "rightly divide the word of truth" if you don't know the word of truth or haven't read it. You see, the bible is a manual for spiritual reformation. So to understand the world of the Spirit, God's world, the place where God resides, we must understand who He is and why He does what He does. We are able then, to walk in the Spirit without fear of mistake. We will know the rules in order that we might follow them. Since we understand that the wages of sin is death, and please know that we are speaking of eternal death, we will be able to escape the punishment by simply adhering to the voice of God speaking through His word.

God takes sin seriously

Another thing we must understand is how serious God is about sin. In Joshua chapter 7 is described the sin of Achan. After Jericho was defeated, the next city in the path of Israel was a city called Ai. Over 3,000 soldiers of Israel were killed and the rest fled from the warriors of Ai and it was because of the sin of Achan. God had told the Israelites that the gold and silver and vessels of bronze and iron were to be consecrated (set apart) to the Lord. But I will let Achan tell it in his own words.

> *Joshua 7:21*
> *When I saw among the spoils a beautiful Babylonian garment, two hundred shekels of silver, and a wedge of gold weighing fifty shekels, I coveted them and took them. And there they are, hidden in the earth in the midst of my tent, with the silver under it."*

Well, who could blame him? A wedge of gold weighing fifty shekels? Two hundred shekels of silver? That's a lot of shekels. But was it worth it? The result of Achan's sin was pretty harsh.

> *Josh 7:24-25*
> *Then Joshua, and all Israel with him, took Achan the son of Zerah, the silver, the garment, the wedge of gold, his sons, his daughters, his oxen, his donkeys, his sheep, his tent, and all that he had, and they brought them to the Valley of Achor.*
> *25 And Joshua said, "Why have you troubled us? The Lord will trouble you this day." So all Israel stoned him with stones; and they burned them with fire after they had stoned them with stones.*

This may seem a bit harsh to those of us who love life. I mean stealing is bad, but come on. The problem here is that Achan was stealing from God and that can lead to serious trouble. God wanted to get His point across to the rest of Israel and sometimes that wasn't so easily accomplished. But the Old Testament isn't the only place where we see God having trouble with sin and sinners.

Jesus didn't put up with sin either

Jesus was no easier on sin than His Father who is described in the Old Testament. Some believe God to be different in the Old Covenant than He is in the New Covenant. He isn't. He is the same as He was 5,000 years ago today. His views about sin have not changed. He said these words during His famous sermon on the mount:

> *Matthew 5:27-30*
> *27 "You have heard that it was said to those of old, 'You shall not commit adultery.'*
> *28 But I say to you that whoever looks at a woman to lust for her has already committed adultery with her in his heart.*
> *29 If your right eye causes you to sin, pluck it out and cast it from you; for it is more profitable for you that one of your members perish, than for your whole body to be cast into hell.*
> *30 And if your right hand causes you to sin, cut it off and cast it from you; for it is more profitable for you that one of your members perish, than for your whole body to be cast into hell.*

When the Lord states that whoever looks at a woman to lust for her has committed adultery in his heart. This means that if you have thought it, you've done it. Whoa! Even your imaginings could be sin? This is a breakthrough moment for many of us. How could it be sin to merely think some thoughts? That's how much power our mind has. The ability to invent sin in our minds is a very dangerous thing. It allows us to visit or revisit our sin without actually being there. Jesus says here that is sin also. Just the visit in our mind is sin. Let that sink in a bit before you go on. Sin is not only conceived in our mind but is perpetrated in our mind as well. As soon as we begin the act mentally, making a plan to sin, even though it may never be conceived, it is sin.

That should scare you a bit. He even recommends plucking out your own eye if it causes you to sin, or cutting off your right hand if it causes you to sin. Both of these seem a bit harsh but that is how serious the situation is. If we fail to realize how deeply concerning sin is to the Lord, then we will never take sin seriously. God hates sin.

Sin comes from hope

This may sound very strange, but it's true, sin comes from hope, albeit a misplaced hope. The addict hopes the drink, the fix, the hit will make things better. News flash; firing synapses and endorphins do not make things better, they just feel better. The rapist hopes he will finally find satisfaction in the act, the thief hopes this will provide what he needs. The liar hopes for either a solution or adoration from this present lie. Hope is in everyone, but if that hope is misplaced then we find ourselves lost to righteousness and walking toward darkness.

Sins of Omission

We should also be aware that we may sometimes sin because of our inaction. As I said at the beginning, that anything not done in love is sin. Love is proven by action, not words. Our failure to demonstrate love when it is needed is a sure sign of hypocrisy. Jesus' half-brother, James put it like this:

James 2:15-19
15 If a brother or sister is naked and destitute of daily food,
16 and one of you says to them, "Depart in peace, be warmed and filled," but you do not give them the things which are needed for the body, what does it profit?
17 Thus also faith by itself, if it does not have works, is dead.
18 But someone will say, "You have faith, and I have works." Show me your faith without your works, and I will show you my faith by my works.
19 You believe that there is one God. You do well. Even the demons believe — and tremble!

Part of loving our neighbor as we love ourselves is to help our neighbors in need. This is not the government's responsibility, but has been taken over by the government in America as well as many other countries, because it is necessary. The church should be making sure that all have food, shelter and clothing. This would be more appropriate than building cathedrals and monuments to architecture that house most large churches today.

We see in the above verses a fact that should frighten you. The demons believe because they are part of that spiritual world of which I have been speaking. They tremble because they have guilt for what they do. There are those who sin who are not even aware that they sin. Does that make them not responsible? I think not. They have not chased after the knowledge that anything not done in love is sin. And when it is withheld from those needing some sort of love, it is sin as well. For by withholding love, you withhold hope and you fail to love your neighbor as yourself. If we see someone in need of any type of love, the situation requires action.

There are many other sins of omission as well. Just use your imagination. But understand that God is a being who is in the business of providing hope to the hopeless. It is when we discover finally that hope is really only found in one place, Jesus Christ, that we can find a pathway to peace, but to do that we must first have an inkling that there is something beyond this existence. If someone is convinced that this is all there is, you're born, you live and you die, then certainly they are without any hope. Every person must at least hope there is more to life than this present life before they can be found searching for more.

So now that we have an understanding of what sin is and how it came to be, let's move on to how it affects us.

CHAPTER TWO

The effects of sin

Gen 2:16-17
And the Lord God commanded the man, saying, "Of every tree of the garden you may freely eat;
but of the tree of the knowledge of good and evil you shall not eat, for in the day that you eat of it you shall surely die."

The punishment of Adam and Eve is something many people have never considered. Adam was cruising along just fine enjoying naming animals, having a great time and God tells him this is all good and I made it just for you. But wait, there's more! And then he made him another being, someone who would be compatible with him, who could speak and walk and talk and be company for him. And their lives together would be amazing. No worries, everything provided that you could ever desire. Peace and tranquility. Now granted Eve didn't hear from God Himself to not eat of that particular tree, but I'm pretty sure that Adam had conveyed the message. I'm sure the tree was special because we know that *When the woman saw that the tree was good for food, that it was pleasant to the eyes, and a tree desirable to make one wise,*

This tree must have stood out from the others in many ways. I have never been able to figure out how you can look at a tree and tell that it is desirable to make one wise, but apparently she could. But as I said, disobedience to God has consequences. The biggest consequence of this decision to attempt to make one wise was death. For all of us. Remember, Cain and Able weren't born until Adam and Eve left the garden. By the way that was another effect of sin on us. No more garden. No one has ever seen it.

Eve had her own punishment; Gen 3:16
To the woman He said: "I will greatly multiply your sorrow and your conception; In pain you shall bring forth children; Your desire shall be for your husband, And he shall rule over you."

Childbirth is going to be painful. No more ribs being removed or forming from the dust of the ground. You will now procreate and it's going to hurt. And what's more, your husband will be your boss. (sin is painful for most wives in this way) Of course in the wokeness of our present day society this is no longer true. This is but another effect of sin in our society, reversal of God's will for mankind. God's perfect plan after the fall was to make the family unit a cohesive spiritual and physical entity. The father was to be the leader, breadwinner and final decision maker, while the wife was to take care of the home. That included a lot, even back at the beginning. Both parents were to join efforts in raising the children with the knowledge of God. Sin has destroyed that plan.

Sin reaches beyond ourselves

Sin will affect not only the sinner but perhaps many down the line and may well reach into the whole of society. This would be most apparent in people like drug dealers whose wares may kill many. But it is not only drug dealers whose sin can trickle down to many. A lie may affect many people. Adultery can affect a family or even extended family. Anger always has an effect on more than just one person. Sin reaches beyond what it is intended to accomplish nearly every time it happens. It has a power all its own. And it has a punishment attached to it by a righteous God who has never sinned, so therefore He is able to be judge. And He declares in

> *Romans 6:23*
> *For the wages of sin is death, but the gift of God is eternal life in Christ Jesus our Lord.*

Punishment for sin is death because a God who is so pure will ultimately destroy any darkness that enters His presence. It would be destroyed immediately by the power of His pure light. We would do well to read the verse prior to this one so we can understand the reward of being free from sin.

> *Romans 6:22*
> *But now having been set free from sin, and having become slaves of God, you have your fruit to holiness, and the end, everlasting life.*

Jesus makes us free

When we were in sin we were slaves of sin. We answered its call each time it sounded simply because we were enslaved. But when we come to Jesus asking Him to forgive our sins, we are washed clean from our old habits and sins and darkness. We no longer require ourselves to answer sin's call. But we must maintain it. The forgiveness of sins is a pretty great thing but unless maintenance is provided, we will soon find ourselves returning to the same place again and again.

But there is good news. The maintenance program to prevent us from falling back into sin is the same thing as the reward for not returning to our sin. It's realizing what Romans 6:22 is saying. We have been set free from sin and now are slaves of God. We must ask ourselves often, what the duties of a slave are. That's fairly simple: To do the Master's will. Oh, that we could figure that one out. We seem to have great difficulty attempting to understand God's will, but it really isn't that difficult. Paul said this speaking to slaves of his day who were believers:

> *Eph 6:5-7*
> *5 Bondservants,(slaves) be obedient to those who are your masters according to the flesh, with fear and trembling, in sincerity of heart, as to Christ;*
> *6 not with eyeservice, as men-pleasers, but as bondservants of Christ, doing the will of God from the heart,*
> *7 with goodwill doing service, as to the Lord, and not to men,*

If he spoke to those who were slaves in his day this way, encouraging them to do their work with obedience to those who were their masters, how much more should this apply to those of us who are free already in this life? But we either fail at doing service for others or we may do it and fail to do it in the name of Christ. Either way it is a failure of our will to do the will of Jesus, which is to love one another

This is simply another effect of sin on we who desire to do well, but fail again and again because of the power sin holds over us. We must never forget two things.

1. Sin has power
2. Sin is powerless against Christ.

Biggest problem with this is that we fail to stay "in" Christ. When we are "in" Christ, when we are within the framework of allowing our life to be taken over by Jesus in all our thoughts, words and actions, then sin is powerless over us. But few maintain this position. This is simply because we are owned by sin. We have been enslaved our entire lives and most of us find it quite difficult to leave that state of sin because we are unwilling to do what must be done. When we fail to understand what it is to be "in" Christ we fail to honor His will. But when we do understand what it is to be in Christ we are rewarded with spiritual, eternal freedom. Romans tells the story:

Romans 8:1
There is therefore now no condemnation to those who are in Christ Jesus, who do not walk according to the flesh, but according to the Spirit.

If you are walking in the flesh you cannot be walking in the Spirit of Christ. The two are incompatible with one another. Romans Chapter eight is a seminar on why we must be found "walking in the Spirit" if we are to successfully overcome sin. (More on that later) Walking in the flesh is one of the results of sin in the world. We are born into this flesh, unaware that we even have a spirit, but God did not leave us in a position of being unable to find either our spirit or redemption for that spirit which has been born in sin. He made it so we would have to seek out Christ, seek out the answers to salvation if we are to be saved. He made it so we would chase after Him.

Pictures of sin

In the 24th chapter of Matthew beginning at verse 45, Jesus paints another picture of sin and the results of it in four different parables which carry through to the end of chapter 25.

The first is about a servant who does well and acts appropriately and the reward he is given, which is becoming a ruler over all the Master's things, but the counterpart, a servant who when left to his own devices, beats his fellow servants, and begins partying with drunkards and it's simply because the Master isn't around. The result of this behavior is being cut in two and appointed a place with hypocrites. I am not fully sure of all that entails, but it doesn't sound like something I would want to have happen to me. And then it says there will be weeping and gnashing of teeth. The result of the sin of hypocrisy sounds fairly extreme, so we would do well to do and act as we profess.

Ten Virgins

The second is the parable of the ten virgins. You're probably most familiar with this one; Ten virgins awaiting the bridegroom. The all have oil, but only five brought extra or enough to carry them through the waiting period. One of the most important parts of this parable is verse 25:5, which states that while the bridegroom was delayed they all slumbered and slept. The ten virgins are representative of the entire church and the oil is the investment each of them has made in the relationship with the bridegroom. (Jesus) It represents their seeking, their discovery of truth and the time they put into the relationship. So this is a time when the entire church has fallen asleep. Look around yourself, at your own community. Is the majority or at least half of the church in your area seem like they are alive? Are they vibrant? Are people attending? In much of the world, the church has fallen asleep. Churches are going bankrupt in America at an astounding rate. This is not a church that is alive, although there are elements of spiritual greatness among us, but many churches are dying all over the world. Praise God for those which are standing strong and standing in the word faithfully.

The five virgins who are prepared with extra oil are those churches, (those people) who have prepared themselves for the waiting. They study the word of God, they pray, and they are aware of the world around them and because of it, they act to show love to those who are in need in any area of life, whether it be spiritual, mental, physical or emotional. These are the ones who have the mind of Christ, whose faith and trust in God will carry them through any situation that may offer suffering and pain. But mostly they trust that God will accomplish what He has said He will.

The five foolish virgins did not prepare. They failed to invest in the relationship, so even though they were believers in Christ, they lived their lives without concern for the relationship. They weren't prepared to wait, so like the servant in the first parable, they took the long wait to mean that it wasn't going to happen. They lost their faith. They are told to go to those who sell oil and buy some for themselves. This oil represents everything I just mentioned…plus; The mind of Christ, faith, hope, trust in God, knowledge of God, but I believe mostly faith. It is the one thing that shows our hearts more than any. Faith is a great thing in God's eyes. Their sin was in not preparing correctly. The result of that sin was not being allowed in to the wedding. If you are one of the brides, that would be horrible. But the result of not preparing for the wedding is not being allowed into the wedding, so prepare!

Parable of the talents

The next parable has to do with the Master who was leaving on a long journey. He decided to split up His some of his wealth between three different servants. Although they were not explicitly instructed to invest the money, by reading the parable you see that was the intent. Make a profit for the Master. The servants represent the church. In the parable, the first servant gets five talents to invest. This representative of the people who are given much to work with. They have many abilities, many talents, and many gifts. They use all of these things for the glory of God and bring many to the kingdom. The first servant has been given much, the second servant has been given less (two talents) and the third only one talent. As I said, the talents are representative of abilities and talents and gifts, and represent their distribution to each of us. But they also represent the investment we are willing to put into a relationship with Christ. The time spent in prayer and study and just awareness of His presence in your life. The reward was commensurate with the amount of success the servant had while the Master was away. Since this is metaphor, we would assume these to represent not merely the number of people you have brought into the kingdom, but also those good works and displays of love you have shown and done that show God's love to others. For with each act of love done in the name of Christ you are able to show someone the kingdom of God. Even a small glimpse is welcome to those who are lost. Some of us have been given much in way of abilities and gifts and a failure to use them is considered sin in God's eyes. Jesus said this in

The third servant hid his talent which he had been given in the ground. He returned the talent in full to the Master with nothing else. He gained nothing for His master. He did nothing to show His Master's love to anyone. He had no faith, no trust in a God whom he professed but failed to project in his life. Yet he professed that he was "of the Master", that he belonged to Him because he was one of His servants. These are the Sunday only Christians or the Easter and Christmas Christians. Just another case of hypocrisy. The result of this sin was being cast into outer darkness. God requires that we show up to help others (love your neighbor) and He requires an investment into His kingdom (love God with all your heart). His second commandment, Love your neighbor as yourself tends to show His commitment to that dynamic. He asks that we use the things with which we are blessed to show His love to the world. It is a sin of omission to withhold His love from someone to whom you are able to show His love. It may only be words of encouragement but that may be all someone needs. Always remember that there are four areas of life in which people may need assistance; Physical, spiritual, mental and emotional. If you provide comfort and show God's love in any of these areas to someone, then, Congratulations! you are doing God's will.

Judgment day

The last parable in this group is that of the goats and the sheep and I would say it is not a parable as much as it is just Jesus telling us what is going to happen. It begins with, "When the Son of Man comes in His glory"… This is a prophecy and it should frighten many of us. He states there is a reward for those who have done the following:

The things these people did have earned them the reward of inheriting a kingdom. That's impressive. And it wasn't because they did these things for others, it was because they did them for Jesus. In their humility they owned the mind of Christ as they performed their good deeds. They sought oil throughout their lives, they invested their talents in doing those things that please God…loving our neighbors.

But, alas, those who fail to do these things will receive everlasting punishment. Why? Why would God punish someone for failing to do these things? Well, breaking the second commandment is certainly a punishable offense.

I've always believed that the Ten Commandments were mostly negative things. The "Thou shalt nots". The only ones which weren't were the commands to make the Sabbath holy and to honor your father and your mother. We were instructed to not sin, but given no way to overcome the sin in which we may have become embroiled. But Jesus gave us two positive commands which He said contained all the law and the prophets: 1. Love God with all your heart, mind, soul and strength and 2. Love your neighbor just as much as you love yourself.

By being purposely vague on the second one, He is instructing us to do for others what we would like to see happen in our lives. That's all. Humans seem to love to attack one another in many ways. This is sin. It is not loving your neighbor to attack them, either in word or in deed or even in thought. But we also sin when we withdraw from our neighbor. We ignore them and by doing so, fail to care for them when they need us. Rejection is completed by failure to even acknowledge someone who is in need. We may not be able to assist them with their physical need, but we can certainly pray for them. And if possible, we can help them find the assistance they may need, even if we don't provide what is needed ourselves. This is the mind of Christ.

It is this mind that always puts others first. Sin whether it is an act of commission (doing what you aren't supposed to do) or omission, (not doing what you are supposed to do) it results in someone being harmed. And it is possible that the only person being harmed is you. But sin always harms us and/or others either physically, mentally, spiritually or emotionally…or all four. Some sins are so horrible to the human psyche that the effects may range to all four areas. When that happens a person will probably need some help to recover from these types of sins. Luckily, no sin is of such horror to God that He is incapable of forgiving it. But we must come through His Son in order to obtain that forgiveness. And it seems as though those who may be trapped in a lifestyle of evil and darkness would not desire to know Jesus. They are probably lost in that lifestyle and it will take a great move of the Spirit to bring them out, and although it is not impossible, it is unlikely. But with that said, many great saints through the centuries have come out of exactly these circumstances and become great warriors for Christ, so nothing is impossible.

Being in Christ

To be in Christ however will take a humility that is difficult to find in those who are bound by a state of sin. If only mankind would realize that it takes only a thought, a single thought, a questioning perhaps about the reality of our life, our situation, or even our direction to begin the path to change. That question may appear out of the very sin in which we are engaged, or it will become a nagging irritation to seek something else by those whom the Lord has chosen. If the Lord has not chosen someone, they will have no such yearning. But that is not to say that they are lost, only delayed. We are not in charge of how or when God chooses to draw people to Himself. Only He is in control of that. And that is why we should never be shy about sharing God's love. We don't know how it will affect them.

Our future is in our hands. When we hear the call and respond it is the beginning of change. Each time someone hears another person speak of Jesus, speak of forgiveness, or speak of God in positive ways, those who hear those words are touched, even if they don't know it. It takes many years and many mentions of Christ to make those who are lost in sin to finally respond correctly to God's urgings. We may not see the change that may be happening or hear the questions that person has, but we will be acting as road signs to direct others to the mind of Christ. Each act of kindness, each display of love brings all of us one step closer to being "in Christ".

Who do you want to be?

When you were young, you had heroes. I'm pretty sure everyone had one...or more. You saw someone throw a pass, star in a movie, hit a home run, be successful in something amazing, break a record, win an Olympic gold medal, win a war, be in a war, challenge something and beat it, or even wear cool clothes, wear a hairstyle you wish you could pull off, drive a great car and a million other things that seem to impress us as humans. I even had local heroes I attempted to emulate, guys who were athletes, or wore their hair in cool manner. I even tried to walk like one guy once just because I thought it looked cool. The people we see doing these things, we want to emulate. We desire to be like them. We desire to have what they have. We want to be like they are because they have a certain suave de fair that we are yet to possess. Perhaps not in way that would make us want to steal what they have, but more likely, just to be like them.

I had a roommate once that was successful at everything he touched. I wanted to be like him in many ways. But we were both involved in the world, so I wanted to emulate worldly things. I wanted success with things that were sinful. I was very successful. I made a hero out of someone who didn't know who Jesus was, so my path was into darkness, even though it didn't seem so bad at the time. My sin swallowed up any previous knowledge I had of the spiritual world and hid it from my mind as well as keeping me from godly pursuits. I became lost in my sins and in worldly pursuits. I lost touch with that roommate many years ago, so I don't know how things turned out for him. I pray he found the Lord.

We all have had heroes. We have all looked to someone and said, "I would like to be a little more like that person. They do things the way I wish I could. They have success like I want to. They are cool." We do this because we find, on introspection, that there is something we don't like about ourselves, something we would like to change. The mirror is a difficult judge indeed. But what if what we are seeing in the mirror is not what is really there? Perhaps not *who* is really there?

The power of sin

When we are in sin, we are affected in every area of our life whether we know it or not. Our spirit is definitely affected, but so is our emotional health, our physical health, and our mental health. We are feeding all of these areas of life with nothing good because we are convinced that whatever it is we do is not so bad. We have succumbed to the idea that our sin is not so very evil and dark. Many others have done a whole lot worse. This is just not important to anyone and doesn't really hurt anyone. This is the mind of a slave. Jesus said this in

John 8:34
Jesus answered them, "Most assuredly, I say to you, whoever commits sin is a slave of sin.

We have already seen that sin has power. We see now that it has the power to enslave us. That's a lot of power. And it's something we do involuntarily and for the most part willingly. We get into the groove and just let it flow. It's very easy to do and we will discuss later methods of keeping that flow from flowing. But how does it affect our image of ourselves to our self? Sin can affect our emotional health in such horrible ways that we can fully withdraw from others, which is quite dangerous from a godly perspective. Sin, all sin, develops in us a sense of both pride and rebellion which removes our humility as well as our concern for others. In this pride we stand before God and tell Him we no longer need Him to direct us. This is how we ruin our lives. God desires we have abundant lives and that means we must both have contact with other humans and provide for those less fortunate. It's built into us. We cannot be fulfilled as humans in the cave. We have to get out and speak to others, touch others, love others in order that we might be fulfilled.

Physically, sin may do great harm. It has that prerogative, but may only do minor damage. Different sins cause different problems, but all sin causes some problems. And continual demonstration of any sin over time will cause physical harm.

Emotions and the mind

As far as mentally, sin can do and always does damage. Our mental and emotional lives are tied together so closely that one cannot be affected for either good or bad without affecting the other. If you feel great emotionally, then your mind will work great, producing positive thoughts and working your way through each day's problems with joy in your heart. But if something happens to trigger an emotionally charged event, your mind reacts to your emotions, your thoughts suddenly turn to another place and your mental state is now challenged. This is also how sin can make us physically ill. Your mind can make you sick.

The transverse is true as well. If you are focused on the things of God and of love, your mind will be centered on goodness and love and will react to situations with joy and love. If your mind is taken to dark places, through any means, visual, through sound, through spoken words, and you stay there, you mull it over and over again, you begin to live in that dark place, so your emotions will follow. Sadly so will your body and your spirit. Your entire soul will live in the darkness. James gave us insight into what exactly is the process to get ourselves involved in a little sin.

> *James 1:14-15*
> *14 But each one is tempted when he is drawn away by his own desires and enticed.*
> *15 Then, when desire has conceived, it gives birth to sin; and sin, when it is full-grown, brings forth death.*

Pay particular attention to verse 14. We are drawn into sin first by our own desires. We are enticed by our dreams. It may not be a great desire, like a desire to rule the earth, but even those types of desires are born out of first, tiny desires. Perhaps you see something you want in the grocery store when you are young. You know mom isn't going to let you have it, but you want it. It's right there. You know it's wrong because you have been told it's wrong to take things without paying for them. But you want it. You watch mom as she turns away from you and you look around to make sure no one else is watching, and you shove it into your pocket.

Desire has now conceived and given birth to sin. That tiny act, that first sin has given birth to a particular type of sin in your life. You have become a thief without even knowing that it was happening. This is the formula to any sin, every sin. Desire forms in your heart or your mind. You are unable to overcome that desire, so you do something, tiny at first, but ever increasing to make that, whatever it might be, yours. It may only feed a sense of conquest or success, and you don't really care who gets hurt along the way, but as long as your desire is delivered to your sense of lust, you remain happy and slightly fulfilled. But in that false fulfillment, you find it wanting and really very empty. This is how you know that what you have desired is sin. It won't really give you the fulfillment you thought it would.

That's because your spirit is trying to break through to your mind. Your spirit can only find fulfillment in one place, the place where all life originates, God. Your spirit (your mind) understands things your brain may not grasp, but it must follow your mind or your will because the mind directs the entire operation, which we will call our soul. But our spirit is crying out for connection with God. It resides in all men. We seek something of which we know nothing and so we seek fulfillment in things or people or places. All of which draw us farther from God. But the sense of want never goes away because deep down in our spirit we know there is more.

Sometimes it makes things really bad

I once lived in the neighborhood in Tacoma, Washington where Ted Bundy, a rather infamous serial killer grew up. My kids went to the same junior high as Ted. I wondered at the time what turned a kid who went to the same junior high as my kids into a serial killer. Was it one of his teachers? Was it a vice principal like I had in high school that tormented me endlessly? No, it wasn't. I read an interview with him after he was caught that begged that question. In the interview, Bundy admitted that when he was quite young he found some magazines while going through a dumpster that were filled with nude photographs of women. That first experience, as well as probably many other excursions into the feminine physique resulted many years later into the deaths of thirty women. At least that is how many he confessed to. His sin touched thirty families forever. God hates sin.

You may think that perhaps, "Well, at least I'm not a serial killer" but I'm afraid that won't get you far in God's economy. Sin is sin and it is my understanding that the wages of all sin is death. We must cease from our sin, but we need not fight the battle alone. God has arranged it so we are able to be victorious over any sin. But we must engage each sin on the battlefield of our mind first and then allow His Spirit to confront us and fight for our righteousness.

Our spiritual image

So, now let us turn to the spiritual side and sin's effects on our spirit. The mirror we hold up to look at our self reflects what our image is physically. Our spirit cannot be seen in this way. But is there a mirror with which we can see our own spirit? It is a spiritual mirror of sorts, but unlike a physical mirror, which shows the exact reflection of what exists in the physical mirror, this spiritual mirror shows us what is missing.

What we may fail to grasp is the fact that as spiritual beings, we desire to be governed by our spirit. When we are involved in sin, of any sort, whether the "tiny" sins like gossip and cheating on a test, or the darker sins of lust and theft and lying, sin has an effect on us. All sin. And as that sin is repeated again and again, the weight of it becomes heavier and heavier. We have indeed become slaves of sin.

Our spirit knows this is wrong. As I said, the sense of want for something more is in everyone. Some are so lost in a particular sin, that finding their way out will take some time. So when you are lost, you need a map. The map out of the darkness of any sin is simply to walk towards the light. What many people, even Christians, do not understand is that God is a relational being. He desires to have a relationship with each of us. And all we need to do is acknowledge that and then act on it. That is the first step. You must truly understand that God has watched you from the moment of birth. He isn't like you. He's bigger, smarter, stronger, and much, much more powerful. He is able to give life and take it with a single word. But in all that power, all that ability, He is filled with love. The bible says He IS love.

And because of that, He desires to have a relationship with you. But you cannot come before such pure love, pure light, the essence of purity with sin on or in you. It will be your destruction. It must be removed. It matters not what your sin may be, it can be removed. But there is only one way. It is through Jesus Christ. Jesus said:

John 14:6
"I am the way, the truth, and the life. No one comes to the Father except through Me.

How does this work?

Since we are unable to be pure, God had to make a plan to make us pure. He would first show us what light looks like, then what it acts like and then how to join it in its actions which are in concert with God's own actions. Once you have seen the light, the pure light of God, you will never desire to return to darkness. For it is in this light that you discover mercy and forgiveness first. That is the moment you come to Christ in a serious manner. This experience is necessary and you are unable to force it, but only God can make it happen. It may or may not involve some exterior sign, but most likely will.

In my own case, it happened in my living room alone after studying the bible for six weeks in an attempt to disprove it and after reading Isaiah 55 and understanding that I wasn't God, but that He was, I fell on the floor and wept for a solid two hours, crying out to God for forgiveness and mercy. I arose from that experience changed in most ways. But I was different and I was thirsty for the word of God. I kept seeking Him. And that is how I know that it wasn't something I did. I had no intention of becoming a Christian and after all, I was attempting to disprove the bible. After six weeks of intense study I came to Isaiah 55 and everything I had read came together in my mind which erupted in my heart and spread quickly to my body.

When one realizes just how evil he really is before a God whose only interest is that person's total and complete happiness, it will cause you to be changed. No malice ever, no evil plans toward you, only complete love and a desire for your happiness. Who would not desire to live in that kind of eternity? You would be foolish indeed to turn from such a wonderful scenario. And what's even more interesting is that once you obtain this position, your desire becomes to share it with first those you love and for whom you care, and then everyone else. Not everyone will want to hear it, but you know it is your responsibility to show it to others.

If you are reading this far in the book, you probably already know what must be done, but in case you don't, I'm going to give you an idea of what you need to do in order to have that experience of which I spoke.

First, just look up and sincerely talk to God like a loving Father and start to tell Him about you. The things you hate about you, specifically. These are your sins; The things that would be disgusting to anyone who is pure. And He is pure. Enter into this place of the presence of God humbly and ask Him for mercy. He is merciful. But you must come through Jesus. His sacrifice, His blood was what makes this mercy available to you. It is all about Jesus. The plan was from the beginning of time, for God operates out of time. And in that plan, we all have a purpose.

Degrees of sin

The Catholic Church teaches that there are degrees of sin; venial sins, which are minor sins and mortal sins which are deadly to your soul. They also teach of a place called purgatory where those who aren't so bad, who have committed no mortal sins for which they have not been forgiven, are placed for temporary punishment until they have been sufficiently chastised for their smaller sins. These are both great ideas, but they are not biblical. Neither of these things are anywhere in the bible.

Man looks at a murderer or a child rapist or human traffickers as some of the most evil people who could ever exist. And I agree. But God doesn't. God says in His word that any sin can be forgiven if the sinner repents from that sin. But he must repent.

> *1 John 1:9*
> *9 If we confess our sins, He is faithful and just to forgive us our sins and to cleanse us from all unrighteousness*

This makes no mention of mortal vs. venial. And in Isaiah God makes this statement about sin:

Isaiah 1:16-20
16 "Wash yourselves, make yourselves clean; Put away the evil of your doings from before My eyes. Cease to do evil,
17 Learn to do good; Seek justice, Rebuke the oppressor; Defend the fatherless, Plead for the widow.
18 "Come now, and let us reason together," Says the Lord, "Though your sins are like scarlet, They shall be as white as snow; Though they are red like crimson, They shall be as wool.
19 If you are willing and obedient, You shall eat the good of the land;
20 But if you refuse and rebel, You shall be devoured by the sword"; For the mouth of the Lord has spoken.

This kind of describes the worst sins (red like crimson) as being made white as wool or snow. But there are qualifiers there. One must become willing and obedient to God's word, which literally means to go and sin no more. If someone is serious about asking for forgiveness from God and they include repentance in the request, they are assured forgiveness for that sin. But they must understand repentance. There will be more in later chapters about repentance, because if you do not understand repentance you will not be able to repent. It may not be what you think it is.

Dealing with temptation

We all have been tempted to sin. All of us. There is nothing to be ashamed of because you have been tempted. Even Jesus was tempted and He was tempted personally be satan. By looking at the temptations of Christ, we can see how we should overcome temptations and refuse to enter the portal of sin. The story is found in the fourth chapter of Matthew.

First of all, Jesus was in a weakened physical state. He hadn't eaten for forty days. Try that sometime and see if you can still walk. He had to be hungry. So the very first temptation he encountered was food.

Matthew 4:3-4

3 Now when the tempter came to Him, he said, "If You are the Son of God, command that these stones become bread."

4 But He answered and said, "It is written, 'Man shall not live by bread alone, but by every word that proceeds from the mouth of God.'"

Jesus' response was to turn the temptation to a spiritual line of reasoning. Jesus was quite aware that He is spirit, but so are we all. When the lust for food attacks, we should turn our spirit free and chase God. Of course, we must eat, but when the desire for food becomes gluttony it evolves into sin. We should direct ourselves more often to spiritual pursuits to satisfy our hunger.

The second temptation of Christ was:

5 Then the devil took Him up into the holy city, set Him on the pinnacle of the temple,

6 and said to Him, "If You are the Son of God, throw Yourself down. For it is written: 'He shall give His angels charge over you,' and, 'In their hands they shall bear you up, Lest you dash your foot against a stone.'"

7 Jesus said to him, "It is written again, 'You shall not tempt the Lord your God.'"

This shows how little the enemy really understands about Christ. This was a temptation of Jesus' ego. We are all tempted with ego at some point in our lives and for some, it is their favorite sin. Jesus could have jumped off that pinnacle of the temple and flown around the area for a few minutes if he so desired. The devil wasn't sure if he had the right guy. He wanted a demonstration. The answer that came from Jesus should have alerted him to the fact of who he was dealing with.

The final temptation was this:

8 Again, the devil took Him up on an exceedingly high mountain, and showed Him all the kingdoms of the world and their glory.

9 And he said to Him, "All these things I will give You if You will fall down and worship me."

10 Then Jesus said to him, "Away with you, Satan! For it is written, 'You shall worship the Lord your God, and Him only you shall serve.'"

This was ultimate control over the earth. But we can relate it to the thirst for power present in many people. It can happen to anyone. I'm sure you have known people whose thirst to get ahead at any cost has caused great turmoil to others. I have and it is a sad thing to see. Climbing the ladder of success over the backs of others is a very mean thing to do and it shows a great lack of kindness. Instead of worshipping money and power, turn that into worshipping God and you will understand true power.

In all these different temptations, we see that Jesus' response was from the word of God. This is another reason why we should involve ourselves in the diligent study of God's word. It is absolutely the best defense against temptations. The Psalms and Proverbs are filled with statements that will drive the enemy away in a heartbeat when they are used. But it is important to note that commanding a demon to leave you is too late once you have lingered even momentarily in the thought of sin. Once you entertain a sin at all, even for just a moment, it can be devastating to overcoming it.

CHAPTER THREE

Our purpose

Gen 1:28-29

28 Then God blessed them, and God said to them, "Be fruitful and multiply; fill the earth and subdue it; have dominion over the fish of the sea, over the birds of the air, and over every living thing that moves on the earth."

29 And God said, "See, I have given you every herb that yields seed which is on the face of all the earth, and every tree whose fruit yields seed; to you it shall be for food.

When mankind was created and Adam was formed from the dust of the earth by God, God did it so that Adam would have a place to be and something to keep him occupied. He gave mankind many gifts. Later, He put us in charge of tending to the earth. Well, we certainly do have dominion over everything that moves on the earth. Perhaps we have not been the caretakers we should have been, but that is another result of sin. Sin takes away from every mission we are assigned and makes it second rate or incomplete.

When God created Adam, He had not yet created the Garden of Eden.

Gen 2:7-9

7 And the Lord God formed man of the dust of the ground, and breathed into his nostrils the breath of life; and man became a living being.

8 The Lord God planted a garden eastward in Eden, and there He put the man whom He had formed.

9 And out of the ground the Lord God made every tree grow that is pleasant to the sight and good for food. The tree of life was also in the midst of the garden, and the tree of the knowledge of good and evil.

So, we don't know what Adam was doing or even where he was created, but only that God placed him in the Garden to take care of it and have a place to commune with God. God wanted a friend. In Gen 2:15 it is stated this way

Then the Lord God took the man and put him in the garden of Eden to tend and keep it.

Adam's mission was tending to a garden that is filled with all kinds of animals which are friendly and did not want to eat him, while all he had to do is pluck fruit off of vines to eat. Not a bad mission at all. I'm not sure what tending included, but since God had planted it, I don't think there was too much to do. Just enjoy living there and every once in a while, trim a bush. Living in paradise though, was spoiled by disobedience to God's command to not eat of a particular tree. This disobedience to God's command was never termed sin, but obviously, it was. God handles sin very well and we know that because He made a way for us to be forgiven for our sins. And He did that so we could share in His wonderful provision for all of us who will simply come to Him the way He intended. Using His system, His formula or utilizing His plan is the only way to enter into His presence. To do otherwise will result in eternal death. Adam was promised physical death since he was a being that was meant to live eternally. We also are eternal beings. Our spirits will survive forever if we are in Christ, but we will suffer eternal punishment and separation from God if we fail to come through the door of Jesus Christ to return to the Father. Our bodies will most certainly die, although they were originally intended to last forever. This is a result of Adam and Eve's sin. We became mortal beings. Adam lived nearly a thousand years, and had many children so the earth would populate, but later we were limited to 120 years and not too many these days make that.

How sin affects our decisions

But God's original intention for mankind was to have someone to have a relationship with Him. That is still our purpose: To relate to God. He understands our needs, our desires, our pain and suffering, our ambitions, our failures and also the intentions of our heart. What more could you ask for in a friend? Since He does understand all of these things about you and He always has your best interests in mind, then why do we not consult Him more often when we are making decisions? If He understands our intentions, and we are in Him, meaning we are living our lives for Him, then why do we not consult Him first and then wait for an answer before we act in any situation? It seems to me that it would behoove us all to do this.

Now we don't have to get carried away, like praying in the grocery store before you buy each item. Shopping would take on a whole new perspective not to mention that you may need a couple of days to shop for your food. But in major decisions, yes, consult God to do things before you do them and then wait for the answer before doing it. The Lord will never lead you astray. He may not answer you in a physical manner, but there are many ways God uses to relate to us: Through His word, through other people, and yes also through direct contact, although this way is very rare. God has contacted me twice in my lifetime and both times resulted in amazing things. The contact was brief and to the point but changed someone's life for good. (See my third book, "Miracle for a Nobody")

We rarely know what is on God's mind, but trust me, He is able to use you for His purposes if you do two things: 1. Pay attention to what is happening spiritually around you and 2. Act on what is happening spiritually around you.

When I said that we are spiritual beings, I meant it. There is a world we are unable to see, yet it influences things that may be happening in our physical realm. And things that are happening in this physical realm can affect things in the spiritual realm. The two are connected and since God is Spirit, I do believe that the spiritual realm is the one we should pay most attention to. But we don't. None of us do. I don't but I am working on it. You should too, because in the end, it will be all that matters.

Using our spiritual awareness to help

When we are aware of our surroundings spiritually, when we stay in that mindset, we will take on an entirely new demeanor. We will look at people differently. We will not look at their outward appearance, but will notice their spirit. I'm sure you have met someone in your life whose spirit shone through past their physical appearance. Perhaps they were filled with joy and gave off a kind of glow that was not present in the other people nearby. I have met some people in my life like that. I have also met people who at the very first moment they entered the room, you could sense evil and darkness. These are people from whom you should keep a great distance. They will cause you problems. but in the same sense, draw near to those who are filled with the presence of God.

Beware

But evil often takes the form of beauty. It can be masked in the most wondrous of things, beautiful things. God is aware that evil attempts to look like it isn't evil. The best trick of the devil is deceit. Jesus said He was a liar from the beginning. So we must be careful of what we decide to allow into our lives. The word "beware" is a word that appears 38 times in the bible in some form. One particularly interesting appearance is in Hebrews. (Not that all appearances should not be viewed and acknowledged) But I would like to look at this one in particular and see why it is important.

> *Hebrews 3:12-14*
> *12 Beware, brethren, lest there be in any of you an evil heart of unbelief*
> *in departing from the living God;*

The author begins by stating that we should be looking out (be aware) both in ourselves and others (being spiritually aware) of an evil heart of unbelief that would depart from the living God. This means someone who is a believer who is leaving the truth in any way. It could be someone who refuses to call sin a sin, you know; those who call good evil and evil good. It might be those who have lost their faith and no longer believe that God is exactly who He says He is. Faith is the largest and most important piece to our relationship with God. He knows we cannot see Him, but if we are willing to have that relationship with someone we cannot even see or be aware of through any of our five senses, then He is willing to reward that. So, He instructs us in a way to overcome that lack of faith.

> *13 but exhort one another daily, while it is called "Today," lest any of you*
> *be hardened through the deceitfulness of sin.*

He is stating here that we should exhort one another which is just another word for encourage each other. And He says that this will keep us from being hardened by the lie of sin. Sin always lies. It promises but never delivers. It is deceitful and those who practice it are deceitful as well. So the way to get past the deceitfulness of sin is to merely let each other know or to remind others and ourselves that God is true, even though we may not be aware of all that He is doing in our life. We may not see what is happening, but we will see the results if only we will wait, if we will only have faith and humble ourselves before a mighty God. And then he tells us how we can hold on until the end of all things:

14 For we have become partakers of Christ if we hold the beginning of our confidence steadfast to the end,

We must maintain our faith. We must remain strong in the face of overwhelming odds and believe that God has a plan for our life. This is our purpose and we should make every effort both to discover exactly what our individual purpose, our mission, our calling, our direction, or whatever term you choose to use, is in our life as well as how we can best accomplish this purpose, whatever it may be to the satisfaction of the Lord. Since He designed each of us, He knows how to best use each of us. Your purpose, if you are in Christ, is to simply show love.

The power of love

Love is more than a silly feeling that makes everything smell better, look brighter, feel wonderful and leads you into dancing around like Fred and Ginger and pulling up tulips as you leap through your front yard. Love is caring and compassion that leads you into action.

It is the exact opposite of sin. And it is what is expected and will be found in those who come to really know Jesus. With love in our attitude toward everyone we meet we will be made ready for the attacks of the enemy. But it must be the love described in 1 Corinthians 13. This is agape love, which interpreted means a love feast. Nice. Without this kind of love in our being, we will ultimately be using a false love to lead us into sin, so we must be very careful to be sure that the love we employ is the love that comes from God. It has the healing power that comes only from God as well as the comforting power that enables us to pass along God's love to others.

CHAPTER FOUR

Sin and the law and grace and faith

Galatians 3:23-24
But before faith came, we were kept under guard by the law, kept for the faith which would afterward be revealed. 24 Therefore the law was our tutor to bring us to Christ, that we might be justified by faith.

We are told in Galatians 3:24 that the law was a tutor. It taught us what sin looked like. But the law of God is much more than merely a tutor. It was there to show us the curse that had been wrought by the sin of disobedience of Adam and Eve. The law picked out a bunch of things that were either offensive to God or would cause harm to our neighbor and showed them to us. And it also showed us how we could do anything *but* love our neighbor. This is the basic law of God, the top ten. We were taught them in our youth. They are found in the twentieth chapter of Exodus. They show us what God is about. He is about love. Many other laws were added to those ten as time went on, but they were for the Israelites to give them structure and an idea of God's power, His authority and His mercy.

Although they teach us that God desires to be first in our lives and He doesn't want us to blaspheme His holy name and He desires we take an entire day and venerate Him, and they demand that we show honor to both our father and mother, they also teach us what not to do to one another so we won't cause harm to one another. But they really do nothing to show us how to accomplish loving one another. The mere absence of malice does not create love. We were left to figure that out on our own...or at least the Jews were. Mankind had to wait a few thousand years for those instructions from Jesus. The law was given to the Jewish people so that they would know how to honor God in their lives. They gave direction. They didn't solve any problems, but they gave guidance to God's people.

Jesus came and said that the law ended at John the Baptist.

Luke 16:16
*"The law and the prophets were until John. Since that time the kingdom
of God has been preached, and everyone is pressing into it.*

Say what? No more law? And then He seemingly argues with Himself
in the next verse:

Luke 16:17
*And it is easier for heaven and earth to pass away than for one tittle of
the law to fail.*

But He explains Himself back in Matthew that not one jot or tittle
of the law would end until

Matt 5:17-18
*17 "Do not think that I came to destroy the Law or the Prophets. I did
not come to destroy but to fulfill.*
*18 For assuredly, I say to you, till heaven and earth pass away, one jot or
one tittle will by no means pass from the law till all is fulfilled.*

Jesus was really just stating that the kingdom of God has now come to earth. He
is what all the prophets were telling us would come. This is fact. It is the plan God
had from the beginning. It's the way of love without any restrictions. Plus, He was
telling us and them that it would be easier for all of heaven and earth to be destroyed
than for the tiniest dot on an I of the law to fail, yet He, Jesus, God come to earth,
has determined that the curse of the law is no more. It is not what those of that day
expected, for they were too attuned to the physical world, just as we are today and not
to the spiritual world.

The curse of the law

You may never have thought of the law being a curse, but Paul did. But, I thought
the law was a tutor? It was. It is. But as I said, it is many things. And Paul wrote this:

Gal 3:10

10 For as many as are of the works of the law are under the curse; for it is written, "Cursed is everyone who does not continue in all things which are written in the book of the law, to do them."

If we live under the law, we are cursed to do all the things stated in the law. That is impossible. It can never be done by anyone. When you attempt to live under the law, attempting to keep from sin, you will fail. And that is because we were all born into sin. We have sinful natures. We were born into a sinful world and we have all sinned at some point in our life. That is because we were trying to live under the law. When the law is present there will be sin. It is guaranteed. That is why Jesus ended living under the law and began the law of faith.

Grace is what it takes

The reason no one got it, other than a small segment of the population, is because the Holy Spirit was not functioning yet. He did not show up on planet earth with great force until Pentecost. And when He did, He brought grace with Him. Now, many people confuse grace with mercy and grace may not be what you think. It is translated from the Greek word Charis:

charis (khar'-ece); from NT:5463; graciousness (as gratifying), of manner or act **(abstract or concrete; literal, figurative or spiritual; especially the divine influence upon the heart, and its reflection in the life;** *including gratitude)* (Biblesoft's New Exhaustive Strong's Numbers and Concordance with Expanded Greek-Hebrew Dictionary. Copyright © 1994, 2003, 2006 Biblesoft, Inc. and International Bible Translators, Inc.)

So grace is, in every sense of the word, abstract or concrete, whether it be literal or figurative or spiritual, it is God, through the Holy Spirit, enabling us to act like God. It is being so under the influence of the Holy Spirit that we are not prone to sin but rather to praise. It is not having control of everything in the universe, but rather to be free from sin and its power so that we are able to show God's love to others in every single facet of our life. Whether it is to someone who has offended us, or loved us, we, with and through the power of the Holy Spirit, are able to love that person, if only we allow it all to happen. But there is but one way to unlock that door to grace.

You gotta have faith

The Greek word hupostosis is an interesting word. It is interpreted by the king James interpreters in 244 different places as either assurance, belief, believe, faith, or fidelity.

But the author of Hebrew gives us the definition in

> *Heb 11:1*
> *Now faith is the substance of things hoped for, the evidence of things not seen.*

Faith is two things. Faith is first a belief in something so strong that you assign it reality prior to its happening or existence or proof that it is. You know it to be true in your heart and there is no way it could be disproved to you. Faith comes many ways, but we all must obtain it individually. There is no way to inherit it, or purchase it, but oddly enough it comes through a place you may not expect.

> *Rom 10:17*
> *So then faith comes by hearing, and hearing by the word of God.*

This means that everyone who has gotten faith has gotten it by hearing somewhere, at sometime, the word of God. Someone told you about Jesus. Someone may have mentioned the law. Understand that Jesus is the fulfillment of the law. So if you are speaking of Jesus, you are telling people the law, the new law. This is God's plan for word of mouth advertising. Just tell everyone you can how Jesus has changed your life. If He hasn't then perhaps you just haven't had that happen yet, but if you persist you will, for it is impossible to meet Christ in a personal way and walk away unchanged. That is how a relationship with God works. It's personal and on a personal level. Just you and the most unique and powerful being in the universe and He happens to be filled with love for you. But you must believe it. You have to trust Him, both that He is there and that He has the power to free you from the sin that enslaves you, frightens you, and controls you.

When you have that kind of faith, that trust, or that belief is when grace is poured out in your life. God will show up in the way you speak, the way you act, and even the way you think. Your compassion will be at level one hundred and your love meter will be off the charts. You won't sin because you are busy loving God and your neighbor.

The two-edged sword of faith

I have heard it described many times by a dear friend that faith is a two-edged sword. On one side it is believing in the unseen, but on the other it is making the unseen believable. That is indeed the way it works. I would add to that, once we sharpen both sides of the sword of faith, we must place it into a sheath of grace. We must trust God first that He is who He says He is and then once that is accomplished allow the Spirit of the living God work in us to shape us into the kind of person who is representative of God, who is holy and pure.

The spiritual Process

Remembering that we are spiritual beings will be pretty important at this juncture. Accessing the spiritual world is not difficult. You need not seek out a guru, a priest, rabbi or any other spiritual advisor. Just close your eyes. God is present whether anyone is aware of it or not. We need not summon Him, He is already there. Direct your thoughts to Him and don't be shy. He desires to hear from you. Speak to Him or think to Him, but have some contact with the God of heaven and earth. And you will find without a doubt that your life will begin to change. But just like the manna that was given to the Israelites in the desert, it is a daily thing.

Praying without ceasing

In the fifth chapter of 1Thessalonians Paul gives us some directions. In verse 17 He encourages us to pray without ceasing. This of course, does not mean that we should spend the entirety of our day on our knees. I'm pretty sure God didn't make us so we could not live our lives. But He does want to be included in our lives. When we're mowing our lawn He has something to say to us. When we are washing dishes, He might give us something. But we must be in prayer mode to do it.

Now, prayer mode, like grace, might not be what you think it is. It is not a time when we must ready ourselves to speak, but rather, it is a time when we should ready our hearts to hear. This is what Paul meant. To pray without ceasing is to be ready to respond to the voice of God at every moment. When you see someone who needs assistance or you have a sudden urge to do something that will help another. These are the times when God is speaking to you. When you see someone, perhaps you already know them, perhaps you don't, but when you feel the urge to mention God or bring up something regarding Jesus, that is God speaking to you and how you respond is totally dependent on how deep your faith is. Do you believe that is God speaking to you? If you do, then do something about it. Don't just sit there. The spiritual world is trying to open a door and by doing nothing when you hear that little voice say, "Do something!" you are locking out some of the greatest experiences of your life.

Staying in prayer mode will awaken you to the reality of the spiritual world which surrounds us. When you remind yourself that God is everywhere it will do great things to your power to resist and overcome sin.

How Faith works

First of all, anyone who has no belief in the spiritual world will not or cannot understand what this faith thing is, even though it is a principle that works in both the physical and spiritual realms, whether you know it or not. Faith is much more active though, in the spiritual realm. I know this because back in the early seventies I had a friend who exercised faith in everything he did and it was all worldly pursuits. He was very successful in everything he did because he exercised the principles of faith. His faith, although misplaced still gave him success. When I became a Christian he never spoke to me again. Perhaps he had made a deal with the devil.

In both the Hebrew and Greek languages the word faith describes both assurance in belief and fidelity to belief. Faith is not so much believing in the unseen as it is trusting in the unseen. I don't worry because I trust that God is the most powerful being in the universe and He has thoughts of me, personally. I don't care who you are, that makes me important. But He also has thoughts of you. So you too, are quite important. Really. But the reality is faith is actually no more than realizing that we are all perhaps a little less important than we may have thought we were.

Remembering we are spiritual beings is quite valuable, but there is something else we need to remember in order that we would maintain some degree of humility; We are created beings. Never forget that. And all created things have a purpose. A hammer needs a nail to complete its purpose. The nail provides the purpose and the hammer completes its purpose in hitting the nail. The nail then completes its purpose by holding two things together. Their faith is complete in that they have accomplished their purpose. That is the end of their faith.

OK, if you didn't like that one, try this: God made angels to serve Him. They are created beings and that is their purpose. They go about their assignments, whatever those may be, as God directs them. They can see Him and they are more familiar with Him then we are. We also are created beings. We don't know much about the hierarchy of heaven, but we know angels have rank and order and free will. But God made mankind very special. We are the only created beings that have both a spiritual and physical embodiment. Two beings in one which are so uniquely joined that nothing but the death of one of them will separate them. Genesis 2:7 states that God breathed the breath of life into man which he had formed from the dust of the earth.

I truly think this is oversimplified, don't you? (in fact the entire creation story in Genesis is oversimplified) I mean really, Psalm 139 states that we are fearfully and wonderfully made. That took some planning and designing and creating. After all, we are God's most unique and wonderful creation… I think, uh, I hope. Nah, we are. We are unique because we are two in one. Angels are only spirit. But God made us both spirit and flesh when He breathed His breath into our nostrils. He brought life through that breath and gave to each one of us life along with His spirit, His life, which is the essence of God giving us many gifts simultaneously.

It's hard to love

OK here it comes, the hard part. Since we are given more, there will be more expected of us. God gave us free will which is the ability to choose. What are we choosing? Well, God desires a people who will both understand the meaning of love and then live within that meaning to spend eternity with Him. He created us so we might come to the understanding that since He has given us life, and since He has shown us love by doing this, we should respond in kind. We love Him because He first loved us. His desire is that we show Him through our actions that we love Him above all other things. He is worthy of that because He alone grants life, but even more than that, He has saved us from some pretty bad things. I know that personally He has saved my life a minimum of four times. Probably more. He has probably saved yours a few times as well whether or not you are aware. That's love. And that is what God desires we learn, true love, not the sticky, ooey- gooey kind of love that mankind makes up. Not the inconsistent, filled with holes and frailties and weaknesses that are inconsistent with true love but rather the kind of love that is described in 1Corinthians 13. That is perfect, godly love.

What is the law?

That is our purpose; To live in perfect love with one another. When Jesus said in Matthew 22:40 that all the law and the prophets were hung on the two commandments to love God with all our heart and soul and strength and mind, and to love our neighbor just as we love ourselves, He meant that everything in your life depends on these two things. All the promises of God to provide and protect and to live in His presence depend on how you keep these two commandments.

Give that some thought, some very deep thought. If you fear God, which you should, simply because you are a created being and He is the creator and as such, judges how you, this most marvelous of creations, who has been given some unique and wonderful gifts, will use those same gifts to show love, either to God out of respect and gratitude for what He has given you or to your neighbor to show God's love to them and perhaps even lead them into the way of love.

Be warned though; We must be careful to show *God's* love, not ours, because He is the One who has provided what you are giving away to help someone else. Even if it's just time, it is God who has provided that time for you. He extended your life for that amount of time to do whatever it was that you did to help someone else and he also provided the resources, be it money or food or whatever. So God should get the glory in all things. This is a part of faith; Realizing that we, although God calls us important, are nothing more than tools which shows the love **of** God and love **to** God constantly. Faith is being faithful to our purpose.

Faith works against sickness and sin

The word faith appears more than two hundred seventy five times in the bible. Forty three of those appearances are in the book of Romans. This book is the great educator regarding the power contained in faith. The word used shows not only the ability to heal but the ability to overcome sin.

The word appears in twenty-four of the books of the New Testament. Oddly enough it does not appear at all in the gospel of John and appears only once in 1 John. So I guess John was all about love and not too big on faith. But we know that can't be true, because he was the only apostle who wasn't martyred. They tried to boil him in oil, but it didn't harm him, so they sent him to an island to live out his life where he couldn't do any more harm with that new age Christianity thing. But from looking at the stories of how faith heals, we will see the power contained in faith.

The gospels are replete with stories of many healings, some entire days spent by Jesus healing masses of people, each individually. He could have stood on a hill with all the people gathered below him and waved His hand and they would have been healed. But God does not work like that. He is a God for the individual and because of that we must each come to Him alone and without assistance. It's His rule not mine. When we cry out to Him for healing, He hears us and responds to our pleas individually. It's because of two things: 1) His love for us, and; 2) Our faith is shown by our ability to access the power found in faith. Let me explain.

One day Jesus was approached by the ruler of a synagogue who was named Jairus. His daughter was dying or dead, but He asked Jesus to come and fix the situation. Jesus said, "OK, let's go!" On the way there was a crowd of people crowding in all around Him making it difficult to be in a hurry, but they progressed slowly. There was a woman in the crowd who had an issue of blood going on for twelve years. She had reasoned within herself that if she could only touch just the hem of His garment, she would be healed. She did and she was. And Jesus stopped the parade and said, "Who touched me?" The woman finally confessed and Jesus just turned around and said this:

> *Mark 5:34*
> *And He said to her, "Daughter, your faith has made you well. Go in*
> *peace, and be healed of your affliction."*

She was healed because of her faith. Jesus said that's all it was. He didn't take credit. He gave the credit to her faith. When they got to the synagogue ruler's house, Matthew tells us in his version that they met them outside the home and said, "Don't bother, the girl is dead." But Jesus said "She's just sleeping." And He spoke this to the girl's father;

> *Mark 5:36*
> *As soon as Jesus heard the word that was spoken, He said to the ruler of*
> *the synagogue, "Do not be afraid; only believe."*

He was telling Jairus to keep the faith, baby. It's good stuff. Just believe that Jesus is able. Able to do anything that is needed. God can make a way. The little girl got up like nothing ever happened.

So, if faith is able to heal, how does it work to overcome sin? Simple. It's the other side of blade of faith.

> *Rom 1:16-17*
> *For I am not ashamed of the gospel of Christ, for it is the power of God*
> *to salvation for everyone who believes, for the Jew first and also for the*
> *Greek.*
> *17 For in it the righteousness of God is revealed from faith to faith; as it*
> *is written, "The just shall live by faith."*

Paul knew that living by faith would keep us from sin. To live by faith means that you are walking totally in the Spirit. Your life is devoted to understanding the full gospel of Jesus Christ. He continued in Romans with another thought;

We are justified by faith

Rom 5:1-4
1 Therefore, having been justified by faith, we have peace with God through our Lord Jesus Christ,
2 through whom also we have access by faith into this grace in which we stand, and rejoice in hope of the glory of God.
3 And not only that, but we also glory in tribulations, knowing that tribulation produces perseverance;
4 and perseverance, character; and character, hope.

Our faith justifies us through our belief in Jesus Christ. And the remarkable thing is that the justifying faith we have opens the door to grace which allows us to have more access to God so we can become even more like Him; In our sense of power, in our sense of peace, but mostly in our sense of love. After all that is the end of things with God, but on the way we will have some trouble. That's what Paul meant in vs. 3. But because we have discovered grace through our faith, we now are able to have great joy in the midst of pain and trouble and persevere through any pain or suffering we may encounter. This will build our character and give us hope.

It's odd that these things occur in this order, but without first having suffering, we would have nothing to overcome and we may never learn to grow a strong character and we would certainly be left without hope. Our challenges are meant to grow our faith. I know that personally, some of the challenges in my life that have been overcome have most certainly been overcome by the hand of God.

All of these challenges come together to make us spiritually stronger. When we experience for ourselves the hand of God working in our life, we will most certainly discover great faith, which will lead to great grace, which will lead eventually to great hope. We have faith in Christ so we have hope in His love and we desire to live in that love for all our lives until we meet Him face to face.

CHAPTER FIVE

How Faith creates hope

Rom 5:5
Now hope does not disappoint, because the love of God has been poured
out in our hearts by the Holy Spirit who was given to us.

There is a certain preparation that takes place in our hearts as we invite Christ to share in our lives. Many Christians remind themselves of this during the season of Advent. It is certainly something to think about. Messiah draws near, the God of Abraham is sending His only begotten Son onto this earth to save mankind, and He's shouting to the world, "Will you listen"?

This is the message He gives us during Advent, (although it is available any time) and it is the message of hope. But hope may be non-existent, because we can lose it and yes we can misplace it. How can this be? How can it be that we who believe in the Lord Jesus Christ could lose hope? Has not He promised us all things? Has not He supplied all things? Let's look at something from His word:

This simple little sentence in Romans speaks volumes to us about how hope in Christ should work in our hearts. First of all, Paul speaks here of hope only in God. And he makes it clear because he knows that hope in man, or hope in one another will disappoint. But those who are in Christ, those who are mature in Christ will never be disappointed.

You see, those who are mature in Christ will never hope for those things which are ungodly. "Lord, I hope you'll make me win the lottery". Or "Lord, I hope you'll give that guy a flat tire because he cut me off." God is not our tool for gaining worldly things or for extracting revenge from those who have harmed us.....no matter how much we want Him to rain down fire on the infidels, He will do as He wants to do, and that He will do in His good time. His purpose in giving us hope is that we will grow in maturity and draw nearer to Him in our understanding of His love. And that's exactly what Paul is saying in Romans 5:5. The love of God has been poured out in our hearts by the Holy Spirit who lives not only with us, but in us. We know that we must begin to prepare a place for Him in our hearts and the primary reason for that is because we need to have Him living within us in order to fully understand the depth of God's love for us.

Hope can cause sin

When He pours out that love into our hearts, we are able to grasp it and then pour it out of ourselves to others, thereby helping them to understand a great mystery, or at least question the mystery of God's love. Hope begets hope. But it's a matter of proper placement. Hope is the reason for sin in our lives. We hope this will make us feel better, whatever "this" is. We hope that the lie we tell will protect us from something we fear. We hope that the thing we just put into our pocket will bring us some satisfaction. We misplace our hope quite often.

Jesus was born to bring us true hope and teach us where to properly place our hope. He didn't have to leave His place in glory and lower Himself to become like us, even born in the lowliest of conditions, but He did. God saw that mankind could not become good, because they constantly misplaced their hope, so He devised a way that even so, we could enter into His presence, but He wanted to show us that His main motivation was love and that His end goal was fellowship with us and so that we might receive the hope of eternal life. And that eternal life is not to be found in this place, at this time. You see, this is not our residence. This is our vacation spot. We are truly aliens here and we find *that* so difficult to believe because all we can see, and hear and touch and smell and taste is right here. And what we can't see and hear and touch and smell and taste doesn't matter to we who are so involved in our lives here. But the universe, the very creation that surrounds us says something different. God requires that we do a little research to find Him because what we discover in Him is so glorious, so wonderful, and so very unimaginable, that it lies far beyond our senses to comprehend.

These are the messages He sends. He shouts, "Look at Me in the flowers, find Me in the stars, discover Me in the very cells that make up this body in which you live. I am found in the heart and in the eye, those things that baffle and confuse you, which no matter how deep you research and study, you cannot understand…and then understand this…I desire you. I long to hold you close to me and take away the pain you feel, to dry the tears you weep and to make you understand those things that are beyond you." These are the things God tells us through not only His presence here now, but through His presence when Jesus came to be with us on that night in a little town called Bethlehem. He could have chosen to descend on this place with glory and an army of angels, plowing their way through the evil and disgusting things that man had wrought upon this earth. But He rather chose to come to us gently and humbly, quietly showing us the life we could enjoy if only we were willing to walk away from the life we endure.

Hope in God does not disappoint

He chose instead to fellowship with us and spend time with us, and He did that in order to explain the way His love works, to show us the merciful eyes with which He looks upon us, and the grace He desires to give to us. The hope He desires we own. No, hope does not disappoint. Hope reveals the love of God and the love of God reveals hope. There are so many things in this world that disappoint us, that give us pain, that are meant to destroy and do destroy our hope. The world is hopeless, while the world with Christ has hope. We cannot expect to have it both ways. We must each remove ourselves from the world as much as is possible if we desire to have real hope. And although we must remain in the world, we must not necessarily be *of* the world. That's where kindness will come in handy. The world and the things in it are not kind. They are selfish and self serving. They depend on greed and malice to further themselves.

Hope does not disappoint because the love of God is able to overcome the greed and malice of the world. Kindness, which is the center of God's love, is able to overcome the evil and selfishness that destroys the human spirit. Hope in Christ is the beginning of kindness and the beginning of the end of selfishness.

Well placed hope is essential

We must, because of this, be very careful of that in which we place our hope, because it is quite possible to place hope in the things of the world. We will find it impossible to have true hope if we do this because the world always disappoints. How often in your life have you hoped for something so much only to find that when it was finally obtained, that it was not at all what was envisioned?

It's like a child who desires a puppy. He sees a cute little puppy that is in a store or somewhere else and they begin the onslaught of asking the parent to allow him to have a puppy. "Can we get a puppy, can we get a puppy?" This may go on for a very long time. The child is filled with hope at the prospect and possibility of getting the puppy. If the parent is wise, they ask the child, "Will you take care of the puppy?" to which the child will always say, "Yes!".

Most of the time wisdom fails in that regard, because the parent doesn't outline exactly what it means to take care of a puppy. There is much more than just feeding and watering which is what most kids think will be the fullness of their responsibility. They fail to ponder exactly what becomes of the food and water after the puppy has processed it. They don't think about how the puppy will need baths and grooming. They have failed to count the cost completely. And to a parent, that is the most important part. And because the child has not counted the cost fully and usually the parent has not either, the parent is often the one who takes care of the after processed product as well as bath time. In this case hope has caused disappointment.

But with Christ our hope is always more than what we could imagine. You see we hear of the love of Christ that is poured out in our hearts and that this love will free us from the chains that bind us and we, being sinful creatures, cannot really understand what that must be like. We don't even understand that we are in chains. We feel just fine. So the Holy Spirit begins His work of showing us ourselves and if we are wise, we one day look into the mirror and see the most disgusting, vile creature we have ever known. So we think back about that which we have heard about; the freedom found in Christ. We hope that it is true, and we invite an unknown entity to take over our very being by the act of repentance and so our true hope begins.

How much does it cost?

This hope does not, and can not disappoint and in fact, will deliver much more than what we at first imagined, but the key is us. Jesus promised many things, the very first being salvation. And that salvation is free, but as I've said many times, it costs you everything, the bonds that held you, the pain of your old ways, the guilt at the things you have done. You will lose everything you once counted as dear and near, because they all belong to the world. To experience the hope found in Christ we must shed the old and run to the new, embracing this newfound life with all the vigor of a child who has finally grasped the ability to walk. But after the walking is developed, the running begins, but we must never return to the old hope, the hope found in the world, for that which is seen may easily replace that which is unseen, especially when we do not have a firm footing or understanding of things spiritual.

That is why it is of great importance that we not neglect so great a salvation as is mentioned in Hebrews 2:3. We must immerse ourselves in His word so that we can come to a true understanding of what that word is saying to us. We must allow the Holy Spirit to do His work and not be dissuaded by events that happen, by trials and temptations that come our way. The enemy is bound to attempt to have us run back into the hope that is the world's by reminding us that we don't have enough; enough money, enough food, enough of this or enough of that. He wants you to place your hope in money and stuff. You will be disappointed.

Don't hope in the world

Jesus said He would never leave us nor forsake us. I would much rather place my hope in Him. I have seen so many things that are beyond my understanding when it comes to the things of God. I have seen the reward of maintaining hope in Christ, of having faith in God. I have also seen the opposite. I have seen those whose faith failed them, and those whose doubt overcame them, collapse on the floor weeping because of the losses they endured simply because of the lack of supply. Their hope in Christ was replaced by their hope in the things of the world.

May it never be. We are Christians and because we make that claim, may our hope always be in Christ. There is no other in which we may find such glorious hope. That doesn't mean that you will not suffer. It doesn't mean that you won't endure some difficult trials, in fact because you claim Christ, you almost certainly will have your faith tested, your hope tried by fire.

When Christ came the first time, He gave hope to billions of people who would follow and understand that this life is no more than a training ground for the practice of God's love that would be shown to all who would receive that love. May we continue in His word, may we continue in the knowledge that we find hope brought by the love of God and then go forth and show that special, incredible, out of this world, passing all understanding love of God to someone else to bring them hope as well.

CHAPTER SIX

Walking in the Spirit

Rom 8:1
There is therefore now no condemnation to those who are in Christ Jesus,
who do not walk according to the flesh, but according to the Spirit.

Many of the New Testament versions of the bible eliminate the last part of this verse. This is found only in the Textus Receptus from which the King James and several other versions were translated. But even if "who do not walk according to the flesh, but according to the Spirit" is omitted, the rest of Romans 8 will convince the careful reader that we must walk in the Spirit of Christ in order to achieve the two-fold purpose of avoiding condemnation and overcoming any sin. Some people, sadly, never read past the headline. But whether or not your version does contain this statement in whole, you should carefully study the rest of Romans 8 in order to understand the complete thought of walking in the Spirit.

But what does it mean, exactly to walk in the Spirit? Well, first of all, notice that "Spirit" is capitalized, so we are speaking of the Holy Spirit, not your spirit. And please notice that being "in" Christ Jesus is further explained by "Who do not walk in the flesh but according to the Spirit." This tells us that not everyone who claims to be "in" Christ Jesus will be walking in the Spirit.

So to begin to walk in the Spirit, you must ask God to guide you. You must go through a period of surrender, whereby you surrender each thing in your personality to Him; Your attitudes, your thoughts, your actions, your words; any issues of which you may be aware such as anger or lust. Everything must be given to God to work with. God is aware of our shortcomings, but this is done so we may become aware as well. We must allow His Spirit to touch even the places in our lives that have never seen light; Our deepest thoughts and our darkest secrets. This should be done alone and with great introspection. Talk to Him and get it all out. Sometimes it will become a wrestling match, but don't give up. Bring everything you can and then ask God to reveal anything you might have missed. He will.

After you have cleaned house, by giving all your shortcomings to God, which is like a complete emptying, it is time to refill your spirit. This process can also be grueling depending on how you have humbled yourself, but it is also quite refreshing. You may be drained, but strangely have great energy.

Hearing God's voice

God will begin to speak to you in order to guide you in loving and kind ways, but in order to discover them you must be listening for His voice. This is the part for the novice that is the most difficult. Since God is everywhere and is manifest in all of His creation, look first for Him there. Begin to look for messages in the words of others. There really are no rules. But pay attention to both what you have read in God's word and what you may hear Him speak to you. His voice may be found speaking both directly to you and also through other's directions for you to follow. You must have great discernment in order to spot the real messages, though, so praying for that discernment will be necessary.

Many things may seem like coincidence, but trust me, God is real and He does use people to do His will…but only those who are listening for the signs from the spiritual side will hear and see the various things God may use. The greatest example of which I am aware happened to me. I wrote of it in my third book, "Miracle for a Nobody" That day was the first time I actually heard God's voice. It wasn't a conversation and it happened in an instant. Just three words, "Pick him up!" Not loud or threatening, but peaceful and comforting. The voice was gentle but firm, so I did what I was instructed. I picked up a hitchhiker, which I never did under the circumstances that were present at the time. (I had a lot of cash on me) Because I listened, three lives were changed forever. God had a plan and I was part of that plan. It felt good. It was certainly one of the highlights of my entire life.

What is needed

Two points: 1.)You must be walking in the Spirit of Christ in order to hear His voice or even capture even the most subtle of spiritual messages. 2.) It must be initiated by God. You cannot make it happen. God will do this only if there is a reason. He doesn't just spout out words with no reason to do it. I have heard an actual voice only twice in my life which I understood to be the voice of God; Once with the hitchhiker and another when I asked Him to give me the original version of the 23rd Psalm. I wanted to hear it just as David wrote it. Through an amazing set of circumstances, within hours I found myself in a room with a grand piano and a tune running through my head that would not leave. I spent hours punching out the tune (because I don't play piano). I didn't even know the words to that Psalm but they came to me. (Interestingly they were in the King James Version, so that's how I sing it.) I know that I had heard the Psalm spoken many times when I was very young, so it is possible that I retained those words. (I would not discount anything) But it is also possible that God knew He was going to give me that song, so perhaps He started giving it to me when I was a child. I sing it at least once every day in order to bring myself closer to God in praise and worship. He is my Shepherd.

Invasion by the Spirit

But that is not the only way God speaks to us. In the book of Acts, there are recounted several occasions where people were instantly invaded by the Holy Spirit and gave signs and wonders immediately. It may have been speaking in strange tongues or some other manifestations. We should not discount these stories. God is able to still perform these signs and wonders in order that He would be glorified. But He doesn't always do it. Some would have you believe that unless you have been given an unknown tongue to speak, then you are not saved. Nothing could be further from the truth. God is able to do anything He desires to do. He is God. But that doesn't mean He always operates the same exact way in each representation of Himself to each person. I have seen many different signs of God showing up other than the speaking of tongues. Overwhelming joy is the most common I have seen, but I have witnessed tongues, I have witnessed people leaping in the air for joy, falling on the floor weeping, dancing, singing, shouting and sometimes just sitting in quiet peace whilst praising God for saving them. All of these things are God's Holy Spirit coming over someone. Jesus put it like this:

> *John 3:8*
> *The wind blows where it wishes, and you hear the sound of it, but cannot tell where it comes from and where it goes. So is everyone who is born of the Spirit."*

God is not bound by any of man's laws for He is the lawgiver. He is the creator and is even over the law of gravity. There is no law that forces Him to do good or to show love, it is merely the way He is. He can be no other way, for love is His mantra, His being, His make-up, if you will. So His Spirit, which is present in every corner of the earth, is available at all times to everyone to show love the instant they are willing to humble themselves before Him and surrender their sins, their shortcomings, and their needs so that they may be freed from the pain that has happened to them.

You may think God is a narcissistic despot bent on making us subservient to Him, but nothing could be farther from the truth. That wouldn't be love, that would be just plain mean and God is far from mean. The reason that we must surrender our sins, seek forgiveness through the sacrifice of Jesus and humble ourselves is simply because if we approach the purity of God's light with sin in our heart, we would be destroyed. His holy light would obliterate any darkness and if that darkness is contained within us, we would be destroyed in the process. God's love will not allow us to approach Him until we have been cleansed by the blood of Jesus. His blood sanctifies us and makes us pure so we are able to be in His presence.

How God's Spirit works with our spirit

Our mind is located in our spirit. Were it not so, then upon our death, as our spirit departs, it would have no mind. I can't imagine a heaven where a gazillion mindless spirits are floating about. Our mind allows us to think, to speak and to learn. Our mind works with our brain to accomplish everything we do in this physical world, but our mind is solely connected to the spiritual world. This is all part of the amazing creation we were made to be. Because both the Holy Spirit and our spirit are spirits, they can communicate. Our spirit is able to hear the Holy Spirit, but because this all happens on a spiritual level, not using any of our senses, it is difficult for the person who has never attempted to seek God to truly understand what is happening. But this is how it works. Unless God calls an audible, we will be unable to use our ears to hear Him. So, we must hear Him in our minds or if you prefer, in our spirits.

It is God's desire that we would communicate with Him. That is why He has given us His Spirit the moment we begin the process. He wants to help us understand His availability to assist us and guide us. Jesus put it like this:

> *John 14:17-18*
> *17 the Spirit of truth, whom the world cannot receive, because it neither sees Him nor knows Him; but you know Him, for He dwells with you and will be in you.*
> *18 I will not leave you orphans; I will come to you.*

Jesus knew that if this did not happen we would be like children lost in a busy marketplace, not understanding just what we needed to do to just exist. He did not want to leave us as orphans. I love that.

If the Holy Spirit had not been given to us, how would it be possible that any of us could overcome sin in our lives? He said here that the world cannot receive God's Spirit. Only those who have turned their hearts toward God and are truly seeking Him as well as obedient to Him are able to communicate with Him by hearing Him. He can hear everyone because God is everywhere. But only those special ones who have chosen to seek and obey God will receive Him, and once discovered, you won't want to let Him go again. In the next verses Jesus gives us a little more information:

> *John 14:19-21*
> *19 "A little while longer and the world will see Me no more, but you will see Me. Because I live, you will live also.*
> *20 At that day you will know that I am in My Father, and you in Me, and I in you.*
> *21 He who has My commandments and keeps them, it is he who loves Me. And he who loves Me will be loved by My Father, and I will love him and manifest Myself to him."*

He reiterates this importance of obedience. This is no accident. The purpose of the Holy Spirit is twofold; first, to keep us from sin and assist us in overcoming the evil that is so prevalent in this world. God loves us so much that He has made provision for us to guide us out of sin and into holiness. That is true love. Secondly, the Holy Spirit is here to show God through us. By teaching us first by showing us love and kindness and mercy and instructing us to do the same to others in order that they may see our good works and be desirous o have that same heart. We cannot do either of these things on our own, so God, in His great love for us, has committed His own Holy Spirit to live within us to assist us, not force us, to live in obedience to His command to love. The decision is ours every single time an opportunity arises to either sin and return to the world or choose to act within the bounds of love and walk in holiness. But if we have surrendered to the Holy Spirit, we will always make the right decision.

We must understand the correlation between love and obedience here. The evidence of our love for Jesus is shown by our obedience to His commandments. He isn't quite done with that statement. He says it for the third time in the next verses.

> *John 14:22-24*
> *22 Judas (not Iscariot) said to Him, "Lord, how is it that You will manifest Yourself to us, and not to the world?"*
> *23 Jesus answered and said to him, "If anyone loves Me, he will keep My word; and My Father will love him, and We will come to him and make Our home with him.*
> *24 He who does not love Me does not keep My words; and the word which you hear is not Mine but the Father's who sent Me.*

Do you see the connection between the Father, Son and Spirit here? As Jesus and the Father are one, also is the Spirit. The Father and Son both are contained in the Spirit. They are all in all. So if the Spirit invades us, the Father and Son have also invaded us. We have the totality of God living in us. In verse 24 He even states one more time that the one who does not love Him does not keep His commandments. If we do not love God first and with everything we have, we will not be able to keep His commandments. We will instead be embroiled in some sort of sin. But when we keep them, we show Him love and He fills us with more of His love.

The result is joy

Joy is what that kind of love creates in someone and it is how humans express the newfound freedom which is located within the love shown by the Spirit of the living God when we discover that what we have learned about God being able to forgive us so we can move on is true. Joy is the natural outpouring of emotion when something amazingly good happens. We can't help ourselves. God built that into us so we would be able to celebrate.

In Psalm 51 David asks God to restore to him the joy of his salvation. And in Psalm 32 he explains the joy of being forgiven for your sin by God. Joy is inherent in God's people and so it is an integral part of walking in the Spirit. It is the second thing listed in the fruit of the Spirit and so it must be found in those who are being led by God. Can you even imagine someone who claimed he was a citizen of heaven but was grumpy and mean and had no joy in his heart? He never smiles, he never laughs. How could someone like that even think that Jesus would recognize him? Believe me, God smiles a lot. He is the most joyous being in the universe, so come on, get your joy on. Joy is found in praise and worship and prayer and conversation with God. When we are thinking of Him, joy should be emanating from us to others.

Consistency

The biggest problem all of mankind has who walks in the Spirit is staying in that place of being in touch with the Spirit of the living God. Brother Andrew's little book, "Practicing the presence of God" is a tutorial on how to remain there, but basically it just involves reminding ourselves very often that God is both with us and in us. God desires consistency in our behavior and He also asks us that our behavior be modeled after Jesus. Just in case you may be struggling with that, so is everyone else who is attempting it. You aren't alone in your struggle. But I can pretty much state unequivocally that to be like Jesus and to remain walking in the Spirit, joy, and consistent joy will be required.

You have help available

I said a few pages ago that God has not left us alone in our quest to be like Jesus. Jesus promised us the Holy Spirit and He has been delivered. But we must request Him to make us aware of His presence. God is always there, make no mistake, but we err greatly by not making ourselves aware of that presence. We fail to consult Him on things, even the small things. That is how we remain in His presence. We consult Him on everything from what to wear, to what to eat, and also what to watch on television. We might also consider asking Him what we should do each day in order that we might grow in our walk with Him. I think He will point us to things that will enable us to show the love of Christ to others and in doing all these things we will be kept from sin. We will be unable to sin because we are engaged with God all the time. I believe that is what John meant when he wrote this in 1 John 3:9

Whoever has been born of God does not sin, for His seed remains in him; and he cannot sin, because he has been born of God.

We won't be able to sin simply because we are involved with God every moment of every day, so sin will be impossible for us. This is truly how someone who is born of the Spirit of God will behave. He will be lost in the relationship with God to such an extent that he will seek Him hourly and treasure each moment that is shared with God both alone and in the company of others because it is only a prelude to what will be happening for eternity in heaven. You will feel as though the kingdom of heaven has already arrived in your heart and the very life you live you are living not for yourself, but for the King of Kings.

Understanding freedom

Many people who begin a walk in Christ will look for new ways to avoid sin. Believe me, it cannot be avoided. But it can be overcome. We are a race of people who are born in sin and we all are sinners, and some very proficient at their sin. Sin is everywhere which means that temptation is everywhere. So then, how is it that we can live within the parameters of 1 John 3:9 when sin is so abundant?

The short answer is we can't. Man is unable to overcome sin without assistance from God. That is the newfound freedom we discover at the throne of Jesus. In his mercy He has forgiven our sin and with His grace He will begin to teach us how we can overcome sin. We know that grace is the divine influence on our heart and the reflection of that influence in our lives. God is very gracious indeed to provide such influence through His Holy Spirit who gently, not forcefully, brings us nearer to Him in both belief and action. He understands that we don't understand, so He helps us to gain that understanding through the means we have available to us. When we first come to the Lord we come to Him in all the humility we can muster. Most people are quite sincere about it when they first come to realize that there is a greater power that exists and He wants to know us and for us to know Him. But temptation comes after a time and we have a choice to make for the first time in a long time. We have been pretty good for a while now and one time, just a moment of returning to that sin won't affect us. We can always go back to the altar and be forgiven again.

Repetitive sin

You need to study a bit more if this is your outlook toward sin. Sin is disgusting to God, so why would you desire to have it even for a moment in your life. Of course God will forgive you, but that is not the point. What if when you were young, every time you did something wrong you made your mother sick. She vomited every time you talked back or didn't do what she or your father asked, and not a quiet little barfing either, but rather a feeling of being overwhelmed with illness and then uncontrolled vomiting. And you knew that what you were doing is what made this happen.

Would you continue to do what made your mother do this? Well God doesn't vomit when we go off on our own, but our sin, however small or seemingly insignificant, does put a partition between God and ourselves. It can be removed, but the sin must go away. John wrote this;

1 John 5:18
18 We know that whoever is born of God does not sin; but he who has been born of God keeps himself, and the wicked one does not touch him.

We know that the wicked one does not touch those who are truly born of God. But when we read that he who has been born of God keeps himself, it becomes apparent that we have a role to play in staying away from sin. We must learn to prioritize things in this newness of life we have found. And believe me it is a new life. I'll get to that in a moment. The word "keeps" in this verse really means to watch or stand guard. And the word "touch" means to take hold of. So, with this knowledge, we can understand the powerful implications of knowing true freedom as well as the implications of being held by our enemy. Paul agrees with John that we each have a role to play in eliminating sin in our lives. We must make choices and those choices may have to be made many times each day. Satan wants your soul and if he can't have it, he will at least attempt to make your life miserable and remove your newfound freedom in Christ as often as he is able. We must choose with the Holy Spirit to walk away from the often-found temptations, no matter what they are. They return us immediately to a state of bondage from which we must once again ask to be freed.

Rom 6:12-14
12 Therefore do not let sin reign in your mortal body, that you should obey it in its lusts.
13 And do not present your members as instruments of unrighteousness to sin, but present yourselves to God as being alive from the dead, and your members as instruments of righteousness to God.
14 For sin shall not have dominion over you, for you are not under law but under grace.

Now we must truly come to the conclusion that sin will not be able to control us but only if we are acting under God's divine influence and allowing that influence to guide our every step. We will be living in the Kingdom of God, even while existing in this world. We must learn to say no to temptations that separate us even for a moment from the leading of the Holy Spirit. That's what it means to be born of the Spirit. We no longer are living under the laws of man, but rather under the laws of God and I believe they are better for all of us, simply because the laws of God are built on love. They say, "Do no harm to yourself or your neighbor, in fact, just love them, even when they don't love you, even if they hate you."

God's laws are better because...

The problem with the laws of man is that although they may keep us from doing harm to one another for fear of punishment, they do absolutely nothing to promote love for one another. When Jesus said to love God with everything you have, all your mind and your strength, He meant that your every thought, word or action should become a new way in which God will either be praised, worshipped or otherwise given the respect due a being who is in charge of every breath you take. And when He said to love your neighbor as yourself, He meant that if you see your neighbor struggling with something, and if it is in your ability to help, then do so. Even if that neighbor is the cantankerous one who always gets angry at you for no reason. Even if that neighbor just cut you off on the road, or perhaps something much more serious. We must not hold grudges for there is no love in that. If we are truly born again that would be sin to us. We will show love to everyone, even those intending harm for us. God will take care of anything in the hearts of those who have caused us harm or even intend to cause us harm. He is the avenger, not us, because to do so would harm another and would not be actions which show love toward our neighbor, so, even if it feels good to us to exact vengeance, we must forgive. It is of God to forgive and that is what the Holy Spirit would always have us do. Those who have harmed us without being forgiven by God will pay the price. We need not worry about it, we should just concentrate on our own relationship with the Holy Spirit of the living God. And so it becomes necessary for us to forgive others every indiscretion if we desire to be forgiven by God.

Born again

I have heard many say different and varying things of what it means to be born again. So for this explanation, I will return to 1John 3:9 but I am going to include the verse before it.

1 John 3:8-9
8 He who sins is of the devil, for the devil has sinned from the beginning.

For this purpose the Son of God was manifested, that He might destroy the works of the devil.

9 Whoever has been born of God does not sin, for His seed remains in him; and he cannot sin, because he has been born of God.

First of all, in verse 8 in the original language, it reads "He who commits sin". The word "commits" is the Greek word poieo which most commonly is translated "abide" but has a wide application and in general means to make or to do. So it can mean to just do one time or it is possible the author's intent was to say to live or abide in that sin. But as I said, one sin is separation from God, so read the entire verse. Jesus came to destroy the works of the devil…and so the next verse. The work of the devil is destroyed when we overcome sin. Whoops. We can't. But how are we to overcome sin when we know it is impossible.

Perfect help

The word "seed" in verse 9 is the Greek word "sperma". Yep! You guessed it. It's where the word sperm comes from. The image here from John is that God the Holy Spirit has invaded you at the moment you divested yourself of the world and came to the Lord in humble adoration asking for forgiveness of your sins. Just like a fetus, He is growing within you in power and bringing you knowledge when you are seeking. It began at faith, the moment you believed. Belief, in God's eyes, holds great power. Jesus told some, "Your faith has healed you", and Abraham's faith was counted to him as righteousness. (James 2:23) So the growth that happens requires something very important we must provide, and that is our will.

Free will

I must admit, at this juncture, that one of the most irritating things I have ever heard is, "Well, I'm a sinner. I sin every day. It's what sinners do." And I heard this from a preacher. I wanted to slap him on the back of the head for that statement. This is a statement made by someone who has resigned himself to the fact that he has no choice in the matter and that he is forced to live in sin by his nature. That just won't wash with God's economy.

Because God has given us free will we must choose to have Him active in our lives. He will not take over and make us robots. We are free to choose what we choose. But knowing this, we must also count the cost. Free will is a booger because it exacts either a price or a reward. There is no middle ground. Yet, it's one of the most wonderful gifts God has bestowed on mankind. But it will lead us to much pain and sure destruction if it were left to man. Because of our sinful nature, our free will is inclined toward sin. Thank God that His plan was to insert an early warning system into each of us who have chosen to believe in Him and His ability to forgive and to lead.

Since God is incapable of sinning and He is now living in you, residing in your body as a guide and instructor in all things God and godly, it would seem reasonable that you are unable to sin. Well almost. If you became a Christian and never sinned again, please write a book! I don't know of anyone who has ever made that claim. But the goal should be to have no sin in your life. Is it achievable? I think so, but it is a battle. Temptations are all around, so the only solution is to move to a cave and not live in this awful world. OK, that's not very practical. There simply aren't enough caves. So let's look at another way.

Resign yourself to the fact that temptations will never cease. So also, each temptation is a battle, and this battle occurs with an unseen enemy. And unless you see sin as the enemy, you will never succeed in overcoming it. The Holy Spirit is in you, Christian, but you must awaken to that fact, especially now, when temptation is near. Summon Him, call out to Him and ask Him to reveal His presence to you. Ask for guidance and for strength to overcome this temptation. And be consistent with this. Each time you are tempted, stop what you are doing and ask God for help. He will. The only caveat is that you must listen. His voice is small and very feint and it may sound like your own voice to you, but here's the test. God's voice will always invite you to righteousness. He will never guide you into sin. He will always attempt to take you away from it. He wants to have fellowship with you and sin separates you from Him, so it stands to reason that He is willing to forgive us our transgressions. But we must, at some point, cease from our sin.

We need His Advocate

We must go back to the beginning of 1 John in order to discover how we can do that.

1 John 1:5-10
5 This is the message which we have heard from Him and declare to you, that God is light and in Him is no darkness at all.
6 If we say that we have fellowship with Him, and walk in darkness, we lie and do not practice the truth.
7 But if we walk in the light as He is in the light, we have fellowship with one another, and the blood of Jesus Christ His Son cleanses us from all sin.
8 If we say that we have no sin, we deceive ourselves, and the truth is not in us.
9 If we confess our sins, He is faithful and just to forgive us our sins and to cleanse us from all unrighteousness.
10 If we say that we have not sinned, we make Him a liar, and His word is not in us.

Everyone sins. This we know. The plan is for Jesus to forgive us via His shed blood, but we must admit our sin, confess that it was wrong and accept that it is forgiven and attempt to not repeat it. And that's the hard part, especially when you know you can be forgiven again and again. (Seventy times seven) God was aware of human nature and the fact that we humans are unable to self-correct well, so He offers a plan wherewith we may be forgiven for sins we have committed, with the intention of not repeating that same sin. When we return, we can also come back to the throne of grace. John tells us of God's plan for we who are weak.

1 John 2:1
My little children, these things I write to you, so that you may not sin. And if anyone sins, we have an Advocate with the Father, Jesus Christ the righteous.

This certainly does not give us carte' blanche to freely sin in any way we choose, but knowing of the mercy of the Father, it encourages us to cease from our sin and return to Him. With the gentle, guiding voice of the Holy Spirit we will be victorious in this most important battle so we can remain permanently within the boundaries of God's presence in every facet of our lives.

The devaluation of truth

In this day and age there are those who live a lie. There are those who would have you believe that they are the pinnacle of relationship with Jesus Christ. They are leaders among men who profess Christ, but in reality are evil, waiting only for those who follow them to fall **as** them.

> *II Thessalonians 2:3-4*
> *3 Let no one deceive you by any means; for that Day (the day of the Lord)*
> *will not come unless the falling away comes first, and the man of sin is*
> *revealed, the son of perdition,*
> *4 who opposes and exalts himself above all that is called God or that is*
> *worshiped, so that he sits as God in the temple of God, showing himself*
> *that he is God.*

I believe that this prophecy is being fulfilled in this day and age in which we now live and each one of us has the potential to be the fulfillment of it. There is a falling away happening right now and it may not be exactly what you think it is. Those who profess Christ yet live their lives outside the parameters of discipleship by living in sin deceive themselves as well as others. They speak words of love but show no love. We are here at the place where the son of perdition is alive and well and living in the temple of God (God's children) and he proclaims that he is God. And they show him to be God rather than the true God because they follow evil and sin rather than show love and follow God's will for their lives. Now this is a very difficult prophecy, both to hear and to understand, simply because, as all prophecies, it can be something we don't want to hear. Let me use another scripture to explain this one.

We live in an age where many who call themselves Christians are living in a state of compromise and hypocrisy. They give themselves the title of "Child of God" or they say that they are "saved", but their actions belie their words, for their actions would indicate anything other than being under the control of the Holy Spirit, which is exactly what happens to a child of God or someone who is "saved". You cannot be a child of God and living in a state of constant sin, simply because a child of God lives in submission to the Holy Spirit and he cannot live in a state of sin. If we are living in a state of sin, and saying we are of God, we are calling evil good, which is exactly that of which Isaiah warns us in the scripture we just read.

Back in the verses in 2Thess, Paul says that the man of sin sits as God in the temple of God, showing himself that he is God. That word "showing" means to show off…which connotes something that is not real. It's just one who *claims* to be God, but the one big difference is that he sits in the place where God should be, the temple.

So we see that we are the temple of the Holy Spirit of God. To live in sin is to fall away from God (and remember that the verse said that the falling away must come and the man of sin is revealed). Now you can see why we must not continue in our sins, for when we knowingly sin and ignore the promptings of the Holy Spirit, how can we possibly have communion with Him?

To do that would be like us telling our own child to not touch the fire and then they put their hand in the fire anyway. Do we love them any less? Of course not, but they must suffer the penalty for their ignorance of our warning. The wages of them ignoring our warning is the pain of the fire. The wages of sin is death. Does that mean that God stops loving us because we sin? Of course not, but it also means that we, because we know the penalty for sin, must also pay that penalty if we choose to live in sin. God still loves us, but we choose to ignore Him. Here's a scripture that sort of outlines the situation:

> *1 Cor 3:16-20*
> *16 Do you not know that you are the temple of God and that the Spirit of God dwells in you?*
> *17 If anyone defiles the temple of God, God will destroy him. For the temple of God is holy, which temple you are.*
> *18 Let no one deceive himself. If anyone among you seems to be wise in this age, let him become a fool that he may become wise.*
> *19 For the wisdom of this world is foolishness with God. For it is written, "He catches the wise in their own craftiness";*
> *20 and again, "The Lord knows the thoughts of the wise, that they are futile."*

God isn't sitting in heaven watching our every move, and waiting to strike, but trust me, He is doing everything He can to let us know that there is a reaction to the actions we take. That reaction may not happen now, but each decision we make will impact us at some point in our life. If our decisions lead to sin, then there will be penalty for that sin. If our decisions lead to righteousness, then the rewards of righteousness await.

Compromise is the destroyer

Compromise is the choice of something apparently better than that offered by the original choice and involves reducing the value of what was originally held. The choice of compromise is almost always detrimental to the one who is making the choice, because to compromise a value that was first arrived at by careful consideration will always reduce the value of the original.

For example: If I spend years holding my marriage in great value, by investing many days of careful consideration of my wife, such as buying her flowers, taking her out to dinner, always taking out the trash without being asked, etc., etc. (Just being a great husband) And one day some little floosie walks in the door and I run off with her, my choice to run off has made the value of my marriage absolutely zero.

The same thing is true of the child who is told by the parent not to stick his hand in the fire. He believes the parent originally, so he doesn't stick his hand in the fire. But one day, he gets really curious and the parent isn't around to repeat the warning. He reduces the value of the advice of his parent to zero and then strikes out to discover for himself if fire really is hot. He soon discovers that the compromised value was a real value and that he shouldn't have put his hand in there.

So it really comes down to mathematics and values. Let's say that God is the ultimate value, 100. There is nothing greater than 100. Total knowledge of Him is worth 100. The problem is that we must gain this knowledge 1 little point at a time. Sometimes the lesson it takes to learn one tenth of one point of knowledge of God is excruciatingly painful, but we desire to learn it. The more we learn, the more we treasure that knowledge.

We have an enemy who is so very resourceful and possesses a great deal of knowledge of God himself, much more than any of us. But his one and only goal is to keep us from our goal of gaining more knowledge of God. Why? Simply because he has already been judged and can never possess what we possess; eternal life in the presence of God, and salvation from a horrible eternity. The only way that our enemy can keep us from our goal is to deceive us and convince us to compromise our values. He must convince us that what he offers us is of more value than this knowledge of God. Now this may seem a very difficult task, because we are very sophisticated beings and we do possess this wonderful knowledge of God. (I believe I am up to 33 points on the knowledge of God scale now.) There is no way this enemy could fool me.

Do you remember that we just read?

1 Cor 3:18
18 Let no one deceive himself. If anyone among you seems to be wise in this age, let him become a fool that he may become wise.

The wisest thing we can do is to admit that we are very foolish indeed. We are foolish because we are ignorant. We gain wisdom by knowledge of God. By not relying on our own wisdom, our own choices, we force ourselves to rely on the choices God has shown us. Lie? No thank you, God has shown me that it not good to lie. Steal? I don't think so, God has shown me that to steal is wrong. Hate someone? I don't want to because God has shown me that to love everyone is to be like Him.

Trusting God's value system

By relying on the value system God has worked out in each and every choice we make, we not only honor Him, but put ourselves on a path that leads to even more knowledge of Him, thereby allowing us to gain in wisdom, strength and power....all good things.

When we compromise any of these choices for good and choose instead those things put before us by our enemy, we devalue all of the knowledge we have gained and tell God, in so many words, "You know, I understand that that you have a better way, but just for a little while, just a little while, I'm going to do this thing that seems OK to me. It's not going to hurt anyone else and it won't be for very long, and you know I'll be back...I just need to get this itch scratched."

It is our choice that brings us to this place and as we stand at the brink of the cliff upon which we have placed ourselves, we jump. We don't understand fully the implications of that leap, but we do it anyway. We convince ourselves that there is some magical rope that will wrap itself around us and keep us from falling all the way down.

There is a rope like that but on our way down, we pull out a knife and begin to hack at it, for we discover that when we compromise one value, it is ever so easy to compromise another and pretty soon, we can forget the original path we were on and look only to the new thing that our enemy has put before us in whatever form that takes. It could be money, sex or power, but in one form or another it will be lust. Lust is merely a desire for satisfaction and it can take many forms. Our flesh is what we desire to satisfy and we lust in many ways to satisfy that flesh. For some of us it's food.

I'm too fat and I am living proof that lust exists. For others, the lust they feel may not be so easy to see. Can you look at someone and know that they have and unnatural lust for money? I don't think so. Can you see in someone a desire for sex that is more than normal for the average person? Probably not, although sexual deviancy always eventually manifests itself in those who own it. And I got news for you, the devil can't see the things you lust for either. But what he can see is your history as well as your present actions. The enemy knows what you have been prone to in the past and once a lust is developed it is very difficult to change.

Strength comes from being born again

That's why Jesus spoke of rebirth. Just as the enemy knows your weaknesses, God knows your weaknesses, but God also knows your strengths and He concentrates on them, but we must cooperate. When we are born into God's family, God takes those strengths and builds upon them. We find ourselves growing stronger in the righteous things **when we do one thing**; submit to His leading. Sometimes that isn't the easiest thing to do. Sometimes it is the most difficult thing to do. But always it is the best thing to do.

So how do we know that something is from the Lord? Even that can be difficult to discern at times. Remember that the devil is so good at deception that he can make something that is evil appear so very good that we can be drawn to it and made to believe it is a gift from the Lord. Do you think that you're too sharp or too sophisticated or too clever or too old or too wise or to young or too innocent to be fooled? Do you think that you have control over your lusts and that no matter what is laid before you, you love God so much that there is no way that the devil can get you to compromise your values?

Are you more at one with God than Adam and his wife, Eve who walked with God in the Garden of Eden and spoke with Him and were the first of their kind to have communication with Him. They were fooled by one who merely asked, "Did God really say….?" and compromised their very valuable knowledge of God for the lust of knowledge of something new. They didn't even know what it was.

Are you closer to God than David who God called a man after His own heart and in one moment of weakness and lust for a woman, had adultery with her and then had her husband killed and then tried to cover up the sin? Talk about jumping off a cliff and cutting the rope on the way down, David's lust spiraled downward into one sin after another, involving more and more people until the entire nation of Israel was put into jeopardy.

Are you wiser than Solomon who was touted as being the wisest man who ever lived, yet during his reign as King of Israel, he turned his back on God again and again in order to chase the lusts of his flesh? Where is the wisdom in that?

It's still about walking in the Spirit

My point is that even though we have a close relationship with God, even though God has imparted great wisdom to us and even though we may spend hour upon hour in prayer and meditation, none of us is exempt from temptation and desire. The desires of our flesh are the things that make it difficult for our spirit to maintain that close relationship with God. That is why we are admonished again and again, time after time to walk in the Spirit and not in the flesh. When we are in submission to the Spirit of God, *we cannot sin*. It's that simple. We cannot compromise because there is nothing we will value more than our immediate goal, Jesus.

When we walk in the Spirit instead of the flesh **at all times**, is when we can say that we have been born again, for we will overcome sin at every turn, we will never compromise what God has shown us and we will fulfill the admonition of 1John 3:9

This Christian life we live is not easy, but it's not rocket science either. It's fairly simple to understand that we need to love God with our whole heart and soul and strength and mind and love our neighbor as ourselves, it is a whole other matter to do it.

I really need you to understand something. I'm not telling you that if you have sin in your life that you're going to burn in hell for eternity... but if you die in your sins and particularly if you are maintaining some particular hidden sin, there's a good chance that you will. God has always left us a way out of the darkness and that way out is lit by His light. The way out is by a close relationship with God that can only be accomplished through a close relationship with His Son, Jesus. He is ever so close to you right now, because He is always ready to hold you up when you stumble and to pick you up when you fall.

If you already possess that close relationship, please guard it in every way you can. Never compromise it, because it is the greatest treasure you will ever own. It is the treasure hidden in a field, it is a pearl of great price. Absolutely nothing in this life will give you more and prepare you for the moment when you stand in front of Jesus to hear Him ask, "What did you do for me?" Don't be deceived by an enemy who will never be able to enjoy the same things you will be able to take you from that close relationship with Jesus. Your enemy wants you to compromise your values each and every day simply so you will never be able to achieve that oneness with Christ that is simply the greatest achievement you can have in this life.

CHAPTER SEVEN

What about forgiveness?

Since man has it in his nature to be sinful, God had to make a way for us to be in His presence without our complete destruction. Since God is pure and in Him is no darkness at all, anything that is impure or dark would be completely destroyed by His glory because light destroys darkness. So you see His dilemma: He wanted to be able to spend time with His most amazing creation but could not because by allowing them in His presence they would most certainly be ended.

He had to manufacture a way to make us clean. He would make a plan and then disguise that plan in the law He had given Moses, His friend. He would show them the sacrifice of lambs and bulls that had one thing in common, the shedding of blood. Blood is the life force of all animals. (Genesis 4:4 Leviticus 17:14). So God was saying that a life must be surrendered and blood must be shed to satisfy the process of purification, but not just any life. It had to be a life that was without blame, without sin. The reason it had to be this way is because it had to be someone who was already righteous and not deserving of death to make a sacrifice of Himself for the rest of us. Well that pretty much leaves out every single person on earth.

God's plan

God loved His imperfect creation and didn't want to destroy it, so God made a plan that included Himself being the sacrifice, along with someone who would also be representative of the human race, a perfect human life for all imperfect human lives. So he made this plan to impregnate a human woman who was of the right lineage. This was done for proof, not all the proof, but a lot of it, so it had to be a woman who had never known a man. God told mankind about the plan through a series of prophets and then performed the plan in a young girl named Mary who gave birth to this child of God just as God had foretold more than a thousand years before. But only those who are seeking God will be able to believe such an amazing tale. The uninspired will scoff and laugh you into derision. The intellectuals will mock. God has already answered those who would dare mock Him. They will be judged on the last day.

God's plan was to make it so that anyone who declared that they were believers in Jesus as the Savior who has come to earth through the way I just described would be saved from a terrible eternity filled with pain and suffering. But we must come through Jesus. This is stated by Jesus

> *John 14:6*
> *Jesus said to him, "I am the way, the truth, and the life. No one comes to the Father except through Me.*

The reason we must come through Jesus, proclaiming Him as the Savior is because He is the only one who was God who became man. He is the one who was pure and yet willingly gave His life as a sacrifice for all of us so we could be purified through His sacrifice. But we must come through that door of sacrifice. There is no other that will work. Not Buddha, not Mohammed not Vishnu or any other manufactured system or proclaimed deity. Jesus is it. He explained it this way so it would be easy to understand. One must wonder why so few get it!

God as man

God wanted to experience life as a man, with all the temptations and frustrations and pain and joy that accompanies being a man. God is filled with joy and He also wanted us to see that joy is the way to get through all the other things. That is just one of the many things God desires for those who would seek Him with humility. We really can come to Him no other way, for the guilty one should stand humbly before the judge. Arrogance will only prove that you are not repentant of the sin you come to confess. And if your heart or attitude is not right as you step before the throne of God, you might as well stay home.

Getting it right

When we come to the Lord we must come, as I said, humbly. I don't think I have ever seen anyone who is seriously asking the question, "Is there more than this?" who is not humbly asking the question. The arrogant will not even ask it, for their desire is to live in and for themselves. They have been blinded. But all it takes for all that to change is to ask that simple question. God desires to be with us, so it doesn't take much to get the ball rolling. It may be a very slow roll in some cases. In my own case, a man and his wife, who was one of my employees, came to our home for dinner one night in 1978. We had been friends with this couple for a year or so, but this man had never mentioned God. I didn't come to the Lord until 1982, but that night I will never forget. He sat down beside me and said a few sentences. He told me that as a Christian, he was bound to tell me about Jesus and how He wanted to save me from destruction. He said He wouldn't bring it up again unless I wanted to talk about it, but he needed to tell me His (Jesus) name and explain simply how the plan worked. And he said something profound. He said, "All you have to do is call on Him and He will be right there. He took only a few minutes to do that.

He told me that he had not told me this before because he knew I was an atheist, but God would not let him stop thinking about it, so he finally did it. I didn't think about it much, for a while, but in the next few years my life was turned upside down by bad choices I had made. I remembered what my friend had said and simply asked into the air, "If you're really real, make it so it's real to me." I didn't know what to ask, so I asked to be shown the reality of God. The next year led me into the darkest hole of my life and I because I had not experienced God or some miracle, I kept going into that darkness. Then one day, I simply looked at my life and thought I know there is no God, because a kind God would not let these things happen, so I will prove it.

Six weeks later, after attempting to use God's own word to prove He did not exist, I fell on my knees and asked God to forgive me for the evil in my life. I never went back to the sins that had brought me to that moment. I was not sure how it worked at the time, but an afternoon of weeping does amazing things for the soul. I was washed in the blood of Jesus in my own living room. And it was a long time before I understood how God is able to do this.

How guilt helps

Have you ever meant someone who never seems to feel guilty? People who litter are like that. They just throw their trash out on the street with no compunction on either how their trash will decorate the scenery or who exactly will be tasked with cleaning up their mess. It is the height of arrogance. One must wonder what else they may be doing without caring. Serial killers are the same. They do not feel guilt at their sin, so they continue in it.

People who are not attempting to access the Spirit of God do not experience guilt and they cannot experience guilt. But if God has touched you in the past, at any time in your life, it is highly likely that you will feel a sense of guilt if you are living within the bounds of some sin. Guilt is a weight that resides in your mind that reminds you of the difference between good and bad. A sense of compunction or regret that accompanies any action is guilt and it is used by God to affect change in us. When we feel guilt at something we have done it means we regret doing it. It may have felt good for a moment, but afterwards the regret is astonishing. We are poured out in our very soul. It's the kind of sadness David explains in Psalm 51. Guilt can be overwhelming if our sin has truly compromised our ability to function. Most sins we regard as tiny and not worthy of bringing before the Lord. But someone who is born again will be just as traumatized by cutting someone in line as they would stealing something from a store. It is all blackness to those born of God. To those born of the Spirit, the tiniest infractions that may spur guilt in someone need to be addressed immediately by being taken to the throne of God in order to be forgiven and your guilt removed.

The power of forgiveness

Forgiveness is an amazing thing when it comes from God simply because it also involves forgetting. God does not remember your sin once He has forgiven it. It's like it never happened. This is because it is healing for your spirit. We see this in all things that God has done. If I should hit you in the face, I may ask for your forgiveness, but you will probably remember. If I slap you again, even if I ask you to forgive me again, and you do, you will still remember me as the one who struck twice.

When God forgives you, He heals you as well. I have seen it in my own life. It is like there was never anything wrong. I think about my past sins sometimes but because I know I have been healed I will never return to my sin. An example of this can be given in the physical realm. My wife was healed from Stage IV ovarian cancer in 2010. The surgery left her with some scars. She has never had a recurrence or any sign of any other cancer. God's healing is complete, but it might leave you with a scar. When your spirit is healed from some sin you have done, the scar will be the memory *you* have of that sin. If you have truly repented, you will remember but not return. God will forgive and forget. There a number of scriptures that bear this out. Here are a couple:

> *Ps 103:8-12*
> *The Lord is merciful and gracious, Slow to anger, and abounding in mercy.*
> *9 He will not always strive with us, Nor will He keep His anger forever.*
> *10 He has not dealt with us according to our sins, Nor punished us according to our iniquities.*
> *11 For as the heavens are high above the earth, So great is His mercy toward those who fear Him;*
> *12 As far as the east is from the west, So far has He removed our transgressions from us.*
>
> *Isa 55:7*
> *Let the wicked forsake his way, And the unrighteous man his thoughts; Let him return to the Lord, And He will have mercy on him; And to our God, For He will abundantly pardon.*

These verses are meant to draw us nearer to God, for if one is to receive mercy and pardon for an obviously flagrant offense, one worthy of punishment, then we should obviously run toward the one offering pardon. But what is required? What must we do? Simply stop sinning, one sin at a time. It may take a hundred trips to the altar to ask again and again, but eventually, you will either tire of the trip or tire of the sin. Your choice is always your choice. But repentance requires ceasing from that sin. There is another verse from Isaiah that tells us the same thing, but with a qualifier and an explanation of both reward and punishment.

Isaiah 1:18-20

18 "Come now, and let us reason together," Says the Lord, "Though your sins are like scarlet, They shall be as white as snow; Though they are red like crimson, They shall be as wool.
19 If you are willing and obedient, You shall eat the good of the land;
20 But if you refuse and rebel, You shall be devoured by the sword"; For the mouth of the Lord has spoken.

Oops! The Caveat

There is one caveat to forgiveness of which we have not spoken. But it is a most important one. We must forgive others every single thing anyone has done to us before we can be forgiven. We must hold nothing against anyone in our heart. We must truly forgive them and let go of all evil feelings you may have for that person. And it really doesn't matter to God what they might have done, just as God is willing to forgive any sin, we must also be ready to do so. He says this in a couple of places, first I will show you the passage in Luke:

Luke 17:3-4
3 Take heed to yourselves. If your brother sins against you, rebuke him; and if he repents, forgive him.
4 And if he sins against you seven times in a day, and seven times in a day returns to you, saying, 'I repent,' you shall forgive him."

This is pretty cut and dried. No matter how many times he repeats the same sin, forgive him. Does this seem familiar?

In Matthew during the Sermon on the Mount Jesus repeats it just after the Lord's Prayer. And it is the only thing reiterated from the prayer:

Matt 6:12-15
12 And forgive us our debts, As we forgive our debtors.
13 And do not lead us into temptation, But deliver us from the evil one. For Yours is the kingdom and the power and the glory forever. Amen.

14 "For if you forgive men their trespasses, your heavenly Father will also forgive you.

15 But if you do not forgive men their trespasses, neither will your Father forgive your trespasses.

This sounds fairly definite to me. We must forgive anyone who has sinned against us. Everyone. This may take some deep soul searching to discover all that we hold against others. Attempt to remember all the grudges you have held against others or things others have done to you and let them go one at a time. Even the most painful things someone may have done to you must be forgiven. It took me three years to let go of one person and forgive them. Sometimes it is quite difficult, but when we consider why this is necessary, it will make sense to you.

Sin is spiritual

Since sin is a spiritual act, so must forgiveness be. When our spirit is embroiled with hurt which has caused anger within our spirit, we are unable to move forward in our spiritual walk toward Christ. He is willing to forgive you everything you have ever done, because it holds you back in your walk toward Christ. So, it is only right that we forgive others so that they may understand the importance of forgiveness in allowing others to move toward Christ. We want now for all to eat the good of the land.

Eating the good of the land means that you will enjoy peace, safety, abundance in your life, but not necessarily this life. Never forget that God is spirit so many of the things of which He speaks are spiritual. He does address the human condition as well, but in this case I believe it is spiritual. Devoured by the sword back in Isaiah 1:20 doesn't sound too pleasant, but if this is referring to a spiritual sword, then we are speaking of spiritual death. I have known many evil people who died from natural causes. At any rate, in the end, all that matters is the spiritual side of things, so it would be best if we pay attention to that spiritual side. The physical will follow, for our spirit remains in charge. Wherever our spirit goes, our body will follow. Sin is a spiritual offense and so it must be handled in a spiritual manner. We cannot address sin by taking a shower. It is God whom we have offended when we sin, so it is God who must forgive our sins. My mom can't step in and explain that I am such a good boy, I shouldn't be punished. God is judge. But good news; He is a merciful judge.

How long is forever?

Psalm 136 declares 26 separate times that the Lord's mercy endures forever. The word mercy in Hebrew is checed (kheh'-sed) and it means kindness, and can even refer to beauty. It is interpreted by the King James translators as either favor, good deed (-liness, -ness), kindly, (loving-) kindness, merciful (kindness), mercy, pity, reproach, or wicked thing.

The most important thing is that this mercy of God's lasts forever, throughout the entirety of existence. It never stops. When He brings anything to you, it is like it has always been there. And His mercy has always been shown to those who will humble themselves and call out to Him for that mercy. When you are in the state of forever all that exists is now. The past is gone, never to be repeated, at least the past of our physical life.

We should begin this process of forgetting our pasts as soon as we come to the knowledge of the truth. The sins we have done in our past have been forgiven when we asked. And all the sins we commit after coming to that knowledge should be fewer and fewer until we have overcome all of them. That is the goal anyway.

Repentance is the mark

Forgetting is not possible without total repentance. Repentance is the Greek word metanoia and it means sincere compunction and regret for something while at the same time reforming your mind to think differently about whatever it is you are repenting from. It is a complex process, and that's why it takes some time and patience, at least most of the time. Sin has a way of trying to come back on us and make us repeat that same sin again and again. It may feel good, it may taste good, it may tickle many of your senses at once, especially with the memory of previous tickles.

With all of that our mind is distracted. It takes no more than a nanosecond, and temptation is present. But here's how it goes away. It's a choice. It is always a choice. Direct your mind toward God immediately. Don't choose to stay in the memory. Don't allow the tickle to happen there, but rather when you arrive at a thought of God, perhaps in the form of Jesus on a cross; The One who died for your sin which you now have an urge to revisit. If that doesn't work, I'm not sure what will. Put yourself in the place of His torturers. The thought of being the one who drove in the nails or placed that thorny crown on His head, punching it into His skull, or the one who stabbed Him in the side should bring you to tears. But that is exactly what happens when we repeat a sin again and again. We are utilizing the blood of Christ to make our sin possible. We are asking God to forgive us because Jesus was willing to die for our sin. But what if we sinned less? What if we did not sin at all? Do you think that possible?

We don't have to sin

Well, according to 1John 3:9 it is most certainly possible. In fact that verse states that someone who is born of the Spirit, (born again) cannot sin because they are born of the Spirit. The Spirit of the living God has entered someone who is born of His Spirit and will always guide that person into righteousness. We looked at 1John 3:8-9 in the last chapter, but I want to speak of it now in the context of repentance and forgiveness. The Father has provided the sacrifice for the forgiveness of sins in the form of His only begotten Son, Jesus.

Probably the most famous verse in the bible is John 3:16 which states:

For God so loved the world that He gave His only begotten Son, that whoever believes in Him should not perish but have everlasting life.

The word "believes" in this verse is the Greek word Pisteuo and it means to put your trust in something. To believe in Christ means that you trust His words to be true, His actions to be holy, and His assignments to each of us to be orders from headquarters. We do as we are told. We, who are His sheep, hear His voice and we respond to it. (John 10:27) We respond to the promptings of the Holy Spirit. That's how you can know if you are born of the Spirit. Your actions are evidentiary. You will exhibit love.

This feeling of freedom from sin gives rise to the new creation. It is the exhilarating feeling of victory. Addicts feel it sometimes immediately and sometimes after a year or two, at least some do. The problem with addiction is, if you are convinced that you will stumble again you may never leave that memory of who you are. That may be a good thing for some, but I think that if instead of bringing up the old man again and again as a memory, the new creation will begin to imagine himself in a new way. Different clothes, different smile, different attitude. All things are made new. This cannot happen without true repentance.

Learning to hate

If we truly desire to never return to the sin that haunts us, we must learn to hate that sin. We cannot allow the tickle to tickle us anymore. We must become sensitive to the damage our sin has wreaked in our soul. It keeps us from fellowship with the God we say has given us new life. But here we are at the old life. That should make you want to scream. We must learn to hate our sin for that reason and that reason only. We can't take God into sin with us anymore. We must resist and be aware that temptation is all around us, but we are guided by the Holy Spirit of the living God and if we listen to Him, if we respond to His promptings the hate we have for our sin and the love we have for Jesus and the sacrifice He made for our sins, will connect to make us go and sin no more. At least that is the goal.

When the hatred we hold for our sin becomes more than the desire we have for our sin, we will cease from sins against God. But it may also take the understanding of how our sin may hurt others. We cannot love our neighbor if we are lying to them or stealing from them or cheating them or lusting after them or getting angry with them over things that don't really matter or committing other sins against them. When we commit any sin against a person, we commit a sin against God. We must repent. And repentance includes the serious attempt on our part to stop doing whatever it is we have been doing that is offensive. And we can only do that by thinking differently about that sin.

Refocusing our desires

In the lives of many, there is desire. Now, desire is definitely a relative thing. The starving child desires but a piece of bread, while the wealthy man desires power. The young executive desires to climb the ladder of success while the unemployed man desires only to have some sort of work with which to sustain himself and his family.

Sharing, Hoarding and Investing

But desire, as we relate it to Christianity should be directly related to need. When we have abundance, it is our human nature to do one of three things. We either share it with those who are less fortunate than ourselves or we hoard it and hide it so that we will have some for later or we invest it so that we can make more from it and then either hoard or share that which we have made or invest what we have gained so that we can do the whole process again. Now this hoarding and investing and sharing can have much to do with the resource itself. If we have an abundance of food, we are more apt to share that with someone simply because it is a renewable resource....that is if we can easily get more. (I'm afraid that there might be little sharing if things get really bad in the future) It also is easily shared because it is necessary to sustain life and by denying someone food, they might die. That's why you see many people with signs that say, "Will work for food". They don't necessarily want to work, but food is good. By asking for the basic necessity of life, they will find many generous folks who will give them something. Usually money, which they probably won't use for food, but the conscience of the giver is clear, they helped.

We are less apt to share wealth. If someone comes to you and asks for a couple of bucks, no problem. Most of us would give anyone a couple of dollars if they expressed a need, say for a meal, such as our "will work for food" guy. But if they wanted a thousand dollars, we would probably ask a few questions. We would be cautious. We had to work for that money, and even if we didn't, (won the lottery or inherited it) it's still mine. We can go through a litany of things we might either give or lend depending on the situation, the person who was in need who desired something from us, and whether the thing desired is a renewable resource.

Now, put yourself in the position of need. Say you were the one who was in need and you wanted to approach someone who had something you desired. If it were lunch, you might have reservations about just walking up to someone and asking them for money for lunch, but if you were really hungry and didn't know how else to get food, you will discover that hunger creates boldness.

Lack may lead to trouble

Enough hunger will even create a will to survive that will sometimes lead to desperate measures, perhaps even criminal measures. When we look at the anthropology or the development of any given situation, the things which led up to a particular criminal incident, we will often discover that many times a series of bad decisions led to the lack of something which led to the desire for something which led to the criminal act itself.

It didn't start out being bad, it just became bad. So is desire a bad thing? Not at all. For if there were no desire for more, there would be no desire to improve things. The status quo would always be just fine. No industrial revolution, no renaissance, no advances in civilization…ever. Desire for more is a good thing most of the time. In fact God has instilled in us a desire for more. In some individuals, the desire is extreme, possibly even uncontrollable. These are the men and women who might even seem greedy, but if we look closely at these individuals we will probably see that rather than greed, they just have initiative, drive, and enthusiasm for what they do.

What sets apart one who is driven by greed from one who has this great initiative is what they do with that which they gain. Do they, hoard, share or invest? Now this might sound like a teaching on tithing and trust me, that's not where it's going, but I want everyone to see that in the desire for things, and in the gaining of things, there are three things that can happen. Hoarding, sharing or investing. In the physical realm, that's what humans do.

There's always more than meets the eye

But what of the spiritual realm? Have you ever considered that those things which we desire in the realm of the spiritual, can also be horded, shared and invested? When we receive things of the Spirit, it is only because we have desired them. Nothing comes in the arena of the Spirit, unless it is asked for. Jesus said "Seek and you shall find, knock and it shall be opened unto you". Actually the correct quote is found in:

Matthew 7:6-8
6 "Do not give what is holy to the dogs; nor cast your pearls before swine,
lest they trample them under their feet, and turn and tear you in pieces.
7 "Ask, and it will be given to you; seek, and you will find; knock, and
it will be opened to you.
8 "For everyone who asks receives, and he who seeks finds, and to him
who knocks it will be opened.

Jesus was referring to those things spiritual. When we have a desire for something spiritual, we have but to seek it and God will grant it. It's a promise. Our problem is often that we get one spiritual thing, have one spiritual meal, quench one spiritual thirst and think that's all we need. We have satisfied our spirit. Where would we be if we don't daily feed ourselves physically? I'm relatively sure that we would find ourselves dead in a short time. Our spirit requires food as well. And although our body can live while our spirit is in a state of death, we will discover that sooner or later our body will be done and our spirit will be in need of life.

Are you born again?

We have already discussed being born again. What do you think it means to be born again? It is for our spirit, not our body that we are born again. If we are not born again, we cannot enter into the kingdom of heaven. Remember the conversation Jesus had with a teacher named Nicodemus one night. Born again is a spiritual thing, and to gain it we must first desire it. It can't happen unless we first desire it. That's why Jesus said to seek it, but when we find it, what should we do with it? We must either hoard it, share it or invest it. Now you might ask how we could invest in spiritual things. Glad you asked. What do you think Jesus meant when He said to *"Lay up treasure in heaven"*? (Matt 6:19-21) That means we invest our spiritual wealth. So how do we do that?

When we invest in the physical realm, we can do it in several different ways. We can buy some property, that in almost every case will increase in value and then one day sell the property for a profit. We can invest in the stock market and perhaps see a return on our investment….or not. It's a gamble. Or we might invest in some bonds or other long term investments that mature slowly but have a generally good record for producing a net profit, an increase from our original investment.

> *1 Thessalonians 3:12-4:1*
> *12 And may the Lord make you **increase and abound in love** to one another and to all, just as we do to you,*
> *13 so that He may establish your hearts blameless in holiness before our God and Father at the coming of our Lord Jesus Christ with all His saints.*
> *4:1 Finally then, brethren, we urge and exhort in the Lord Jesus that you should **abound** more and more, just as you received from us how you ought to walk and to please God;*

So to invest our spiritual wealth, it also involves taking what we have gained, putting it into a place where it can gain interest and a return. Here it is: We invest in the things of the Spirit by two ways. Love the Lord your God with all your heart, soul, strength and mind and love your neighbor as yourself. You probably thought I was going to tell you to give all your money away and reap your reward in heaven. Let's look hard at the verse we just read. (v.4:1)

The word "abound" in borh vs. 4:1 and in 3:12 is not a word that means to have a little bit extra.

4052 perisseuo (per-is-syoo'-o);

from 4053; to superabound (in quantity or quality), be in excess, be superfluous; also (transitively) to cause to superabound or excel:

94

KJV-- (make, more) abound, (have, have more) abundance (be more) abundant, be the better, enough and to spare, exceed, excel, increase, be left, redound, remain (over and above).

It means to have a whole bunch more than what you need. It is a derivative of the word that means to have extra but it means to have a whole lot more than what you need.

But look closely at verse 12. He isn't speaking of having stuff or money or sandals or anything physical that you can use up. He's speaking of love. And what kind of love is it? It's agape love, not phileo, not eros, but agape love, the kind of love which God uses toward us and who should we love like this? One another. And Paul must have shown them this special agape love, because he says just as we do to you. When Paul first came to Thessalonica, he brought with him Silvanus and Timothy.

It's all about love

And in the first part of this letter, he reminds these people how these men loved them. They weren't a burden to them and they served them with much love. In fact in:

> *1 Thessalonians 2:7-12*
> *7 But we were gentle among you, just as a nursing mother cherishes her own children.*
> *8 So, affectionately longing for you, we were well pleased to impart to you not only the gospel of God, but also our own lives, because you had become dear to us.*
> *9 For you remember, brethren, our labor and toil; for laboring night and day, that we might not be a burden to any of you, we preached to you the gospel of God.*
> *10 You are witnesses, and God also, how devoutly and justly and blamelessly we behaved ourselves among you who believe;*
> *11 as you know how we exhorted, and comforted, and charged every one of you, as a father does his own children,*
> *12 that you would walk worthy of God who calls you into His own kingdom and glory.*

Paul and Timothy and Silvanus certainly showed love to these people. Interesting, but why? Why did they show love to people who they didn't even know and why should we love one another with this kind of love of which Paul speaks, this agape love?

To understand this we must go back and look at 1 Thessalonians 3:13.

So that He (God) may establish your hearts blameless in holiness before our God.

What he's speaking of here is an investment. When you plant love, you reap love. Jesus said that we reap what we sow and Paul is simply reminding us of this fact. When we invest love in a place, in a person, in all with whom we come in contact, the interest we gain is so magnified, so increased that we can easily say that there is no investment that reaps such great rewards.

In 1 Thessalonians 4:1 Paul wanted them (and us) to know that we have the ability to abound more and more. To have so much more of the love that we show is given back to us by God, If not now, in the next life. Invest in love. If we keep this love, if we hoard this love, by never giving any away, we not only do disservice to others, but to ourselves. Love is of necessity of no value unless it is spent. If we sit in our room and keep all the love we have to ourselves, never sharing it, never giving it away, there really exists no love.

Paul understood that if we live a life of sharing God's love with all we encounter, each day giving away the Gospel of peace, the Gospel of love, the Gospel of the promise of eternal life, there will be no time for sin to enter into our lives. In the rest of this letter Paul begins to show another way in which we may abound and it is the way of abstaining from sin. The way he approaches this is so skillfully done. Rather than screaming about repenting and attempting to frighten the sin out of these people, telling them what they must *not* do, he merely tells them what they *should* do.

It's the same approach that Jesus took when, instead of dwelling on the ten commandments, which mostly say Thou shalt not, He concentrated on the two which He said contained all the law and the prophets, love God, love your neighbor.

It takes action

Jesus knew that if we would just do these two simple things, we would never have the time or the inclination to sin. Love is a time consuming, a life consuming thing. When we give our love to God completely, He returns it to us…with interest. That enables us to give it away to someone else who is hurting, who needs some love, who in turn, after they have learned of this love can also go through the same process.

How much is enough love? And how powerful is love? Well according to Rom 8:38-39

> *38 For I am persuaded that neither death nor life, nor angels nor principalities nor powers, nor things present nor things to come,*
> *39 nor height nor depth, nor any other created thing, shall be able to separate us from the love of God which is in Christ Jesus our Lord.*

That's powerful. The love of God is the most powerful force that exists. It is the light that destroys all darkness. It is the all consuming fire that completely annihilates all evil, yet leaves the pure gold of holiness to be cherished by those who know of its value. It is that love that never judges, yet always instructs. It is the love that suffers long and is kind. It doesn't envy, doesn't parade itself and is not puffed up. It never behaves rudely, doesn't seek its own it isn't able to be provoked and it thinks no evil. It doesn't rejoice in iniquity but rejoices in the truth. It bears all things, believes all things, hopes all things and endures all things. Most importantly, it never fails. When we are loved like that, we can achieve all these things. When we love others like that, we help them to achieve all things. How much is enough? There's no limit. There's no end to God's love, to the love of Christ and so from His example we should understand that we are to always share His limitless love with others, just as someone shared it with us.

Love is a prayer, a communication that is spoken through us from God to another. In this same book, this first letter from Paul to the Thessalonians in chapter 5, verse 17 Paul tells us to pray without ceasing. I firmly believe that means to love without ceasing. We have the opportunity daily to do just that. Never let it escape you. Never let an occasion evade you to sow love, for in that you will reap a reward that is out of this world and you will be kept from your sin by becoming lost in the love of God.

CHAPTER EIGHT

Overcoming Sin

OK, so you've had a good time in your life and now you are wondering if this is all there is. There must be more. You think of yourself as a pretty good person, no saint of course, but you try to help when you can and you don't hate anyone, but you have been having this nagging feeling that it isn't enough. If there is a God, what is He thinking about you? Does He even think about you? Probably not.

This is the mindset of much of not only the world but, some, maybe most of the church. But this is not the mindset of a true believer. I said at the beginning of this book that we must come to the understanding that we are spiritual beings who are living within a physical experience. It is not the other way around. We are spirit and unless you have fully embraced that concept, you will never be able to overcome any type of sin, even the smallest. Spiritual beings have a different outlook on sin than do those who are physical beings, unaware of the spiritual side of their own life. They lack peace. So I will assume that if you read this far in this book then you have a grasp on the spiritual world and believe that to be truly living in holiness, you must walk in the Spirit of God.

The importance of peace

The word peace in Hebrew is found as number 7965 in the Strong's dictionary. It is rendered thusly: shalowm (shaw-lome');or shalom (shaw-lome'); from 7999; safe, i.e. (figuratively) well, happy, friendly; also (abstractly) welfare, i.e. health, prosperity, peace:

I've never met anyone who did not desire to live in peace.,.or at least that's what they said. But, I have met some who by their actions spoke something else. They spoke discontent, war, malice, anger, and frustration. They said that they hated these very things, but they constantly did the things that brought all of these things into their lives. I speak in the plural, they, because I have known more than one person who is like this. I have known many. In fact, I may have known more who are like this than those who have truly spoken and then lived in peace. How can this be? How can anyone truly desire anything but peace in their life? How could someone want to live in turmoil?

The answer is really rather simple. They are being deceived. And please understand something; deception doesn't have to be permanent. And to be deceived, it doesn't have to be a really big, huge, giant deception. And it isn't usually the person's fault who is being deceived. Sometimes a very small deception will wreak great havoc in one's life. Of course the big ones count as well and should be avoided, if possible, but trust me; our enemy focuses on the very tiny deceptions in order to throw us off and to remove us from the presence of the Lord. And if he is successful enough, he will succeed in driving us completely from God's side. The way he does this is by destroying our peace. He does that by distraction, irritation and confusion. It may sound like something that we, as mature adult Christian men and women, would easily be able to spot and then overcome. But if we were, there would not be the separation from God that is so prevalent in our society today.

We remove ourselves from Him

And we must understand what causes this lack of peace is our separation from God. There is no other act that can so totally destroy the perfect serenity we call peace as leaving the presence, even momentarily, of the One who grants us that same peace we enjoy by His very presence. And how is it that we leave His presence? We walk into sin, and by this we turn our backs on His great love and away from His great light and run toward the darkness of our own pleasures. I know this to be true because He has promised to never leave or forsake us. So if ever we feel abandoned, it is not God who has abandoned us, but rather we who have abandoned God.

Think about it. When we are close to God, we feel secure and comforted, no matter what is going on in our life. We could be experiencing great pain, but if God is a big part of our life, then the comfort He gives us is much more than the pain we endure, no matter where that pain might be, physical, mental, spiritual or emotional. (Or all four) But if we remove ourselves from that presence, that comfort, and that security, then we feel lost and alone. It never fails.

Those who have never experienced the incredible warmth of His presence, seek out that comfort and security in other ways. They may seek out the things of the world, the wealth of the world or they may try to discover that peace in drugs or alcohol. And that's one of the things I meant when I said that our enemy uses little deceptions to take our peace form us. "One little drink won't hurt you" is what he will say to an alcoholic. "It's just one pill, it isn't addicting" he will say to an addict. "Go ahead, put it in your pocket. No one will know" he will speak to someone who might be a kleptomaniac.

God's presence protects us

All of these things are true. One drink won't hurt you. But I never met an alcoholic who could have just one drink. One's too many and a thousand's not enough is what they say at AA meetings. And let me assure you that if someone has a problem with an addiction, *the* enemy isn't his only enemy. In fact, you become your own worst enemy. Once you leave that place of peace, that place of "shalom", by stepping away from the comfort and protection of God's presence, and please understand that it may be for but a mere moment, it's like jumping over a wall that blocked your view of what was on the other side of that wall and, once you jumped, discovering that you are standing in the midst of a pit of hungry lions. Oops! It's too late. Your peace is gone. Your safety is gone. And here you are in the midst of angry lions. But you see, these lions are different. They don't want to hurt you...yet. They know that if they can keep you from the presence of the Lord, if they can bring you back into the things that are temporary, they will have you for eternity. Then they can torture and hurt you forever. So they offer you comfort, worldly comfort. They have no peace to give to you, so they offer you what they can. On the night Jesus was arrested in the garden, before He and His disciples had even gotten to the garden, He was telling them what was going to happen, that He was about to leave them. But in His proclamation, He reassured them that they would have peace, because the Spirit of the Father would be with them.

John 14:23-27

23 Jesus answered and said to him, "If anyone loves Me, he will keep My word; and My Father will love him, and We will come to him and make Our home with him.

24 "He who does not love Me does not keep My words; and the word which you hear is not Mine but the Father's who sent Me.

25 "These things I have spoken to you while being present with you.

26 "But the Helper, the Holy Spirit, whom the Father will send in My name, He will teach you all things, and bring to your remembrance all things that I said to you.

27 "Peace I leave with you, My peace I give to you; not as the world gives do I give to you. Let not your heart be troubled, neither let it be afraid.

In this very small piece of scripture is found the most amazing recipe. It is the recipe for peace. It's the way to discover what every man and woman desires in their life, whether they are aware of it or not.

Look at verse 23. In this first part of the recipe, Jesus tells us of the evidence that will be apparent if someone says that they love Him. It's the most basic ingredient. They will keep His word. What is His word? Love the Lord your God with all your heart, soul, strength and mind and love your neighbor as yourself. Those are His commandments. Jesus said that those things encapsulate all the law.

So why is it important that we do this? Why is it important that we love Him? Simply because if we love Him, then the Father will love us and the Father AND the Son will come to us and make their home with us. Now it seems to me that if we have the opportunity to have the Light of the world and the Father of light living in us, it would be, at the least, a pleasurable experience. It would be pure peace and absolute safety. In verse 24 Jesus makes a cut and dried statement. If you don't love Him, there will be evidence as well, you won't keep His words. Then He lets us know that this is not His rule, but the Father's.

Then He does something very important. He reminds the disciples that He is telling them these things right now, while He is present with them. He knows that in just a little while, their peace will be taken from them. He doesn't want them to freak out over the circumstances that are about to take place. He wants them to know that their peace will return to them, because He will return to them.

In verses 25 and 26, He is saying. "Look you guys, I've said a lot of things to you. And I've shown you lots of things, but wait, there's more. I'm going to leave and I don't want you to worry that you won't know what to do. My Spirit, the Holy Spirit of God, the essence of the Father and Myself is going to come to you and remind you of everything I have spoken. No worries.

Then comes the capper. I'm leaving you peace. And it isn't just any ordinary peace. It is the peace of God, you remember, the peace that passes all understanding. It's not like the world's peace that comes for awhile with possessions and creature comforts. It's not new chariots, new tunics, gold, or silver and it isn't anything in this earth. It is a peace that is only found with the Spirit of God, Who is not resting within us, not sleeping while we do all the things we desire to do, but guiding our life by means of gentle encouragement and love. Here's the catch. If we say we love Jesus, we must keep His Word by loving God and loving our neighbor. This is not done with mere words, but by actions. These actions encompass deeds that will show the love of God to both our neighbor and ourselves and will eliminate those things we do in our lives that show we do not.

Want peace? Do three things. First, surrender to the Holy Spirit in both word and deed. A submissive heart will be required. Secondly, love God.....with all your heart. Seriously. Third, love your neighbor just as you love yourself.....And yes, it's OK to love yourself. I have spoken of this before and stated that it is virtually impossible to love God and love anyone else if you don't love yourself, forgive yourself, treat yourself as though you were a child of the King.

The real circle of life

Are you seeing the big circle here? Love God, but if you don't love yourself, you can't love God. If you don't love God, you will have no peace. If you don't have peace, you can't love yourself.....or God.....or others. No Shalom. No safety. No peace.

Now, please understand that I'm not telling you that when you are obedient to God that life will be simple and prosperous and that God will supply anything you ask. God's best people, God's favorite children go through some pretty devastating trials. But you see, they know how to endure these trials, with God. They enjoy God's peace while they endure the trial. The enjoy fellowship in the Spirit with the Creator.

Well, you might say, if that's the case why would I want to be a follower of Christ? If I'm going to have to go through the pain anyway, why not just endure it with all the things I like doing, getting drunk, smoking dope, running with wild women? That may bring me some peace where I don't have to endure any trials. Sadly, it just doesn't work like that. All people endure trials, tribulations and suffering; Those who know Christ and those who don't. The rain falls on the just and the unjust. I can guarantee you that it is much better to endure pain and suffering with Christ in your life. I have done both.

T.S. Eliot, who was not really known for his spiritual works, once wrote: "To believe in the supernatural is not simply to believe that after having lived a successful, material and fairly virtuous life here on earth, one will continue to exist in the best possible substitute for this world, or that after living a starved and stunted life here, one will be compensated with all the good things that one has gone without: it is to believe that the supernatural is the greatest reality here and now."

What he means is that if we really believe in God, if we believe that there is eternity, then that will be demonstrated by living as though we were in eternity right now. Do you think that God will meet you when you get on the other side and say, "Oh you sure went through a lot. And because you did, all the evil things you did after you came to knowledge of me don't matter. Your eternity begins now. Here are some fabulous prizes. Show him what we have for him, Peter"

Do you really think this is all there is?

Your eternity is in progress right now. This is just the first stage of it. And the first stage is a relatively short piece of the whole. But what you do on this side of that eternity affects the second part. There are those who believe that this is it. Nothing more at all exists beyond this life. How sad for them. I certainly do love this life, but it gets tiring, and it can wear you down. I believe in a life after this one, one on the other side of the veil of death because God has shown it to me in His Word. I have had some supernatural experiences that were events beyond what could have happened in a natural way. They were events that happened at times in my life while I was truly seeking God uninterrupted. No distractions from the world, even though I was still very involved in the world.

But had I not experienced those things, I would still believe in life eternal. I would still believe in God as our Father and Jesus as our Savior. Why? Simply because He has given me shalom. He has given me the Peace that surpasses all understanding and it is an awesome thing.

Now I can't say that I don't run from the shelter of that peace occasionally, but I manage to reside there most of the time. Just don't cut me off in traffic.....or one of a few other things. But God is working on me. It is a bit funny really. In the worst of situations, when really awful events happen to me, I can keep my calm, not get upset at all and maintain a cool head throughout the ordeal. But if some so and so dare tread into my lane too closely, I'll let him know he shouldn't have done that and not always in a nice way. Perhaps that is because I can see him, I know who did it. In many of life's calamities and disasters, there is no one to blame and 9 out of 10 times, we just need to take the blame ourselves.

Did I do that?

Because when you sit back and analyze most of the difficulties in which you find yourself, you'll discover that they are self inflicted. I know that's not a very popular view in this day and age, but it is true. And the self infliction comes from living outside the shalom, the peace, the safety, the guidance of God's wisdom.

When we truly trust God to guide us, to show us the path which we should walk, when we consult Him in prayer over not only the major decisions of our lives, but the small decisions as well, and then wait for His answer, we will live our lives in the greatest peace imaginable. We will still make our own decisions, but the ones that really count, the ones that help us to love God with all our heart, soul, strength and mind and to love our neighbor as ourselves will be done in the wisdom of the Lord of lights. And that, my friend, is Shalom.

This peace will greatly aid you as you struggle with principalities and powers. You will need it. The battle is far from over.

The great struggle

Eph 6:12
For we do not wrestle against flesh and blood, but against principalities, against powers, against the rulers of the darkness of this age, against spiritual hosts of wickedness in the heavenly places.

It is important to understand that this battle is in a realm, a place we cannot see nor visit, but there is much going on there all the time. If you could look down and be able to view all of New York City at one time, you would see much movement of cars and trucks and trains and planes and people, all happening at once. Now if you could look up and suddenly see the spiritual world, you would see that there is much movement there constantly as well. There is no night time, so the action never ceases. There are battles, and intrigue, and suspense, just as here, but this world of the supernatural is an eternal place with no clocks or even a sense of time. It is always now. That doesn't mean that there aren't events that will happen as well as those that have already happened, but since there is no end of things, now is the most important. This is a concept that you may struggle with understanding. But is the truth of what happens.

The powers that exist in that world, who are from the spiritual realm are much more powerful in their world than they are in this world. They understand that God has the final say in all things, but has ceded His power to satan for a while on this earth. Heaven is still controlled by God and in fact, so is earth. God will retake this earth when Jesus returns to rule. That is according to the word of God. We know the end, but satan will not go easily. He does not believe that he will be defeated even though he has read the prophecies as well. But it is like the Junior High School football team taking on the Pittsburgh Steelers. There isn't much hope for a victory of one so weak compared to God. And that is why our enemy cannot be silent. His desire is to make as many of those who profess Christ to deny Him in their lives. It is his only strategy for winning souls. The ones who do not profess Christ belong to him already.

satan wants your soul

The only way our enemy can get you to cooperate with him is to convince you of two things. That God doesn't really care if you sin and that sin will not have a negative effect on your life. In this way he will convince you that you are free while he holds you in bondage. That's a pretty neat trick. The battle is on every single day, but there are many who will never see the deception in their own life and that there is even a battle which ensues. We struggle to become free from sin and eventually just give up and figure that we will just go to the Lord and ask for forgiveness rather than overcoming the difficulty of temptation. It's a perfect plan.

And it's perfect because it's partially true. God will forgive you. We are assured of this:

> *1 John 1:8-9*
> *8 If we say that we have no sin, we deceive ourselves, and the truth is not in us.*
> *9 If we confess our sins, He is faithful and just to forgive us our sins and to cleanse us from all unrighteousness.*

But this in no way condones sin. In fact the entire book of 1 John is a seminar on how to understand sin and the ramifications of calling yourself born again. We have looked at this verse already, but I cannot emphasize enough how important it is to us:

> *1 John 3:9*
> *9 Whoever has been born of God does not sin, for His seed remains in him; and he cannot sin, because he has been born of God.*

That sounds like someone who doesn't sin to me; someone who has overcome the temptations which are common to all of us. Being born of the Spirit of God is what it is to be born again. Do you really think that God would be drawn into sin by any temptation? The person who is born of the Spirit is allowing the Spirit of the living God to direct their thoughts, their emotions, and their actions. This person understands that it is not themselves who are operating, but rather have ceded operations to God. It is their choice, using their own free will to make this choice. It is a conscious thought process that prayerfully asks God to move in. And then it is a conscious act to allow God to guide each thought and when a thought comes that is brought to this person that is offensive to him/her, then he will immediately turn his thoughts to Christ and away from the temptation.

The power of temptation to sexual sin

Temptation can happen in a micro second. Always be aware that your enemy in this war has been watching you since you were born. And although he is unable to force you into anything, he can certainly tickle your fancy. His most popular tickle is what makes mankind feel the best for a brief moment. Yes, I'm speaking of sexual sin. God abhors sexual sin because it is a manifestation of evil that shows up in one of the most sacred of all the gifts God has given us. Sex was meant to be between a man and a woman so they could procreate. They would learn how to love by this wonderful gift of a child who came from an act that was conceived by the mind of God. And sexual deviation and adultery completely insults the entire process.

God's invention

Think carefully how the process unfolds. A single cell is formed from a single sperm cell from a man entering into an egg that is provided by a woman. This entrance immediately begins the process of physical life. The cells begin to split and replicate at amazing speed. Everything necessary to be the perfect combination of mother and father is contained in the DNA structure that is present when these two meet. The way we look, the way we even think is present in our DNA as well as many personality traits that will lead others to exclaim, "The apple doesn't fall far from the tree." We are who we are made to be. No one is sure when our spirit enters into the picture. I personally believe it is at the very moment that sperm and egg come together. Life is formed and in that life is a spirit.

So perhaps you have an understanding now of why sexual sin is so abhorrent to God. It perverts the intention of the most precious of gifts that God has presented to mankind, reproduction. When we make another one of ourselves we are proving the existence of God through life that has continually been carrying on since Adam and Eve in the exact same manner. It is the invention of God and we should not mock God's inventions by treating them as though they have no value.

When you are tempted with sexual sin, it is imperative that you capture the thought immediately and turn your thoughts to God. The instant the thought takes hold and you give it any amount of time you will find yourself in a hopeless battle to overcome and most likely you will succumb. The key is to do it immediately.

> *James 1:14-15*
> *14 But each one is tempted when he is drawn away by his own desires and enticed.*
> *15 Then, when desire has conceived, it gives birth to sin; and sin, when it is full-grown, brings forth death.*

Understand that because this is not dotted with exclamation points and capitalized as though it was someone screaming at us, I think it should be. We should read this with a sense of urgency to understand it. We are drawn away by our own desires. We entice ourselves unto temptation. Whatever it is we lust for creates in us a desire to have that thing, that person, that idea, that is what we want. And there may be many. So when something that we have expressed desire for (even to just ourselves) comes along and our mind awakens to possibilities of our possessing that, we roll it around for a moment to try first to experience it in our minds and then we act. But read that last phrase of verse 15. When it is full grown, when it is complete (even in your mind) it brings forth death. Sin is death. And this death of which he speaks is spiritual death because sin has already caused physical death for all of us.

Nothing you can conceive in your mind, nothing you can do in your life is worth spiritual death. It is complete separation from God as well as punishment and if not dealt with, will be eternal. We are always welcome at the throne of mercy, because God's mercy endures forever. But we must learn to repent.

Repentance is key

One day Jesus was told about some Galilean people who were killed and Pilate had mixed their blood with the pagan sacrifices. Jesus had this response:

Luke 13:2-3
2 And Jesus answered and said to them, "Do you suppose that these Galileans were worse sinners than all other Galileans, because they suffered such things?
3 I tell you, no; but unless you repent you will all likewise perish.

It is quite possible you may not understand repentance. I have heard that it is a "turning around" and so it may be, but the word used is the Greek word metanoeo and it means to think differently about something. So the most important part of overcoming sin is to look at it from a different perspective. When you look at sin from God's perspective, you will have an entirely different attitude toward sin.

God's perspective is that when we are living in any kind of sin we are not only blocking God from being near us, but we fail on three points. First we are not loving God with our whole heart, mind, soul and strength. Secondly, as already discussed, we cannot be loving our neighbor while we are sinning against him. And that is not just the ones we sin against, but also any of sin's collateral damage. Lastly we are walking quickly away from our mission of making disciples of all men. Always keep in mind that God's mature person is one who shows love at all times. Not worldly love, but God's compassionate and caring love. This love is what creates disciples for Christ. When we are in the state of sin, we are unavailable to love. It is not possible to be in sin and show God's love at the same time. Any sacrifice is tainted by the darkness of sin. We are demonstrated this by the Old Testament sacrifices that required an unblemished lamb. This is all part of understanding the need to look at sin from God's perspective.

A new concept

So as we begin to think differently about our sin, our mind will begin to comprehend and overwhelm our flesh. Our desires will begin to change and our actions will follow. This is why repentance and truly understanding what it is, is so important. We must view our sin, our shortcomings, even our entire life from God's point of view if we are to truly walk in the Spirit of the living God. Also understand that this is a process, not an event.

The greatest need is to be sure that we are patient. God is very patient or I can assure you that we would have all been dust a long time ago. To grasp a new concept is difficult. I can remember when I changed political parties. It was a struggle for me. My father had always been one party and so was I. "The working man's party" I can still hear him say. One day I began to think differently about that party and switched over to one that I thought truly was a working man's party. But it was a struggle. I anguished over it, because it was change. It was different.

If changing a political party is difficult, how much more difficult is it to admit your sin completely to yourself as well as to God and decide that something that has been a part of your basic personality your entire life is no longer needed and that it is an impediment to your relationship with God? So you desire to now change it and you speak it aloud in prayer. Buckle up, buttercup because the moment you declare that you no longer desire this sin anymore, the enemy of your soul, the one has tempted you every single time, is coming for you. And he's going to test your resolve. But, as I said, this is a process. You may return to your sin, and it does not matter what that sin is. Sin always involves one or more senses, sometimes all of them. God is aware.

How our senses work in sin and repentance

Our senses were all made to enhance our life and make it more enjoyable. With them, we can view a beautiful sunset and enjoy its amazing beauty that occurs nightly. We can smell the wonderful aroma of baked bread or our favorite dish and feel awash with memories from the past at the taste of that same dish. We can quiver at the gentle caress of someone we love and we can hear the sweet sound of birds singing in the trees on a spring day.

All these wonderful uses of our senses are the God-inspired gifts that He has given us in order that our lives would be pleasant. These things have nothing to do with the world other than they all exist in each of our own worlds. We are unique in both our discovery and competence of each of our senses. It is totally dependent on our minds and our sin. For example, if at an early age, a young man was taken with a particular style of music or a particular musician, even though the music he liked was dark and evil and he had a talent for the instrument needed, (probably a guitar) he might become proficient in playing that style of music, even though it may be something that honors darkness and evil.

If that same young man somehow had a vision of Christ and his heart was changed so that he became a disciple of Christ, his music would turn from darkness to light because his mind has begun to think differently about the spiritual world and how his own life fits into this newfound line of thinking. He has been captured by the Holy Spirit.

You can utilize any scenario. Any of our senses can lead us into sin. They are all able to be co-opted by our mind and used in a manner not originally intended. When we say our mind plays tricks on us, it's true. Inside our mind is imagination and that imagination can lead us to sin faster than a double black diamond ski run…and with about the same possibility of braking.

So to overcome our senses that are activated by the temptation that comes calling for us, we must employ the same mind that is able to take us into sin. We must train our minds to think of that moment, that instant just before we break free of the gate into sin and turn our mind elsewhere, preferably toward God, Immediately, without hesitation. This is why it is a process. This is not an easy thing to accomplish and it is also why God has made a way for us to be forgiven through the shed blood of the perfect sacrifice of Jesus while we are in process. He knows our weaknesses. He knows our strengths. His desire is to help us complete the project successfully. It is the perfect plan to make the imperfect slowly but deliberately perfect. But the only way it is possible is that we become disciples.

"Christianity without discipleship is Christianity without Christ"

This quote from Dietrich Bonheoffer is one of the truest statements ever made. In much of the church today, in America especially, it is thought that a one time commitment that includes a walk down an aisle, a statement that you are sorry for your sins and perhaps a shedding of tears qualifies you for passage past the pearly gates and into the kingdom of God. You are now free to do whatever you want without retribution or punishment. I am fearful that much of the church will have a very sad awakening on judgment day. That walk is only the beginning. It is the start of a journey. The great commission from Christ is a call to make disciples.

> *Matthew 28:18-20*
> *18 And Jesus came and spoke to them, saying, "All authority has been given to Me in heaven and on earth.*
> *19 Go therefore and make disciples of all the nations, baptizing them in the name of the Father and of the Son and of the Holy Spirit,*
> *20 teaching them to observe all things that I have commanded you; and lo, I am with you always, even to the end of the age." Amen.*

This making of disciples is a lot different than just telling people about Jesus. That is the first step, but He describes the next step in the next verse, "teaching them to observe all things that I have commanded you". Well that is an extensive list. But it mainly instructs us to teach others how to love God and others like Christ. That is what a disciple is, one who follows his Master so closely that it is obvious to whom he/she belongs. And the most important thing a disciple does is to teach by example.

Jesus taught by example and so should we. That is a matter of showing love at all times to everyone. Mercy, compassion and love toward all is our mission.

Discipleship is a lifelong process

Discipleship is not something to which there is a goal, a finish line or a completion. There is no diploma. It is your life. It begins with the understanding that you know nothing of Christ yet desire to learn all that you can and live within the confines and restrictions of what you have learned from the Holy Spirit. The process begins at the moment you discover that God is God and you are not. That simply means that you realize that there is indeed a God and that He loves you. For some this is too difficult, and that is sad. For nothing should be put in front of your desire to be with Jesus. I didn't say it; He did…a couple of times. Here's one of my favorites, though;

> *Luke 14:26-27*
> *26 "If anyone comes to Me and does not hate his father and mother, wife*
> *and children, brothers and sisters, yes, and his own life also, he cannot*
> *be My disciple.*
> *27 And whoever does not bear his cross and come after Me cannot be*
> *My disciple.*

Now obviously Jesus doesn't want us to hate our father or mother or anyone for that matter. This Greek word miseo means hate but by extension can mean to love less. I mean, didn't Jesus say that we should love our father and mothers? So it wouldn't make sense for Him to say we must now hate them. But many people forget the second part there. We must bear our cross. Now, that can mean a couple of things as well. It can mean to endure one's burdens or it can mean to complete your mission. Either way, He adds "and come after Me" as a condition of becoming a disciple. This is no accident. To be a disciple, we must "come after" Jesus. We must chase Him with an attitude of shaping ourselves in His image. He is our hero. He is our desire.

If this is not your attitude, you are not a disciple. You are something else. You are a familiar with Jesus, perhaps an acquaintance, but you cannot be a disciple, for a disciple follows hard after his master.

Jesus cares about your inner life

The whole discipleship thing may seem a bit too much and some would consider it punishment, but it is not so that the disciple is punished, It is so that the disciple loses his or her close connection to the world and a reconnection of his spirit with God. This is what true discipleship entails. We must come to the realization that because God is unlike any other being, to be with God in a close relationship will be unlike any other relationship, so we must give up our ideas of relationships and look solely at this one with an understanding that He is superior in every way. He is smarter, stronger and has power that is unbounded in human terms. He is the creator of everything we can see, touch, smell, hear or taste….and everything we can't.

So who do you think would be better at guiding a relationship, you or God? So, why wouldn't we desire to be in a relationship with a being like that, knowing that He is love, and love is not one of His attributes, but it is His total makeup? He offers peace, fulfillment in this life as well as the next, comfort in times of trouble and forgiveness for every evil act you have ever done. And lest you forget He *will* judge every single person who has ever lived.

So to make this disconnect from the world He offers us a program. Yes, a discipleship program and it entails changing you from the selfish, lying, cheating, stealing, corrupt person you may have been to a someone who has love in their heart, joy in all they do, peace in their being, patience in all things, kindness toward everyone, goodness in their general makeup, faithfulness in all their promises, gentleness in their demeanor and self-control in their actions. And all of these things will occur in every area of life; physical, spiritual, mental and emotional. Of these four areas, three are considered inner life. Your mind directs everything so we must make the first thing we seek the mind of Christ.

Love is the mind of Jesus

How can we make showing love to all mankind the desire of our heart? That's easy. We start with the first person we see and offer them love. People may think you have lost your mind if you do this, so enjoy it. I promise that if you make a concerted effort to be kind and considerate and patient and loving toward everyone with whom you come into contact, your world will change dramatically. People will actually begin to smile when they see you coming. Next add joy to your personality. No matter what is happening in your life, consider daily the miracle of salvation and how it has been brought to you. If that doesn't make you joyous, then you should see someone for help. Add each of these fruit of the Spirit, found in Galatians 5:22-23, as they come to you and are made available. Consider these nine things carefully, for they are the things that will show up in a disciple's life. It may take many years for them to be fully apparent in your life, but if they are present, they are the chief indicator or evidence of Christ in someone's life, the most important evidence of a new creation.

While our mind is being trained to think differently about life we are also training our emotional and spiritual side simultaneously. As we learn gentleness, our anger at small things will be tamed. Our emotions slowly begin to heal. Our spirit yearns to draw nearer to the Spirit of the living God so it is not difficult to bring your spirit to Him. Your own spirit will cry out for more of God once you have exposed it to God. God has instilled that in our very personalities, but in some it is buried very deep.

Peter's discipleship program

Peter wrote a great discipleship program and it's found in his second epistle. It is found in

2 Peter 1:5-10
5 But also for this very reason, giving all diligence, add to your faith virtue, to virtue knowledge,
6 to knowledge self-control, to self-control perseverance, to perseverance godliness,
7 to godliness brotherly kindness, and to brotherly kindness love.
8 For if these things are yours and abound, you will be neither barren nor unfruitful in the knowledge of our Lord Jesus Christ.
9 For he who lacks these things is shortsighted, even to blindness, and has forgotten that he was cleansed from his old sins.

This is another way of looking at a stairway to heaven, or at least heaven on earth. Peter promises at the end that if we do these things we will never stumble. The Greek phrase for this is ou-meé ptaíseeté pote and it means you will never, ever, in no manner stumble. Peter was overloading the phrase with "nevers" so it would be understood that the way to overcome your sin is to do these things; Start at faith, believing in a God you cannot see, then add virtue, which is making morally right decisions, then add knowledge of God, which will take time for study, then add self-control. Please notice that many of these things are found in the fruit of the Spirit as well. Once you have mastered self-control, learn to persevere. Keep doing all these things then add godliness to your own personality. Then add love for your fellow humans and then to that add agape love.

Peter's formula ends at love which is where Paul's list of the fruit of the Spirit begins. I suppose as long as love is at both ends then we will be fine. Peter put very high on the list, knowledge. I couldn't agree with him more. Knowledge of God is found in the word of God, His Bible. But that isn't the only place. You are seeking knowledge as you read this book or any other with the subject being God. But be careful what you read, simply because the enemy is able to write books too. And they may be different or they might be quite a bit of truth with just a couple of lies thrown in. Be diligent in researching the truth. If you read something with which you disagree, I hope you will contact me so we can discuss it. Remember that Peter instructs us to be diligent to make our call and election sure. He knows what it is like to be fooled. If Peter was fooled and he walked with Jesus for three and a half years, then it is possible we could be fooled as well. Check everything you read against the bible. You will be glad you did.

Self denial in discipleship

This scripture in Matthew can be some pretty scary stuff. Those four little words in the middle, *"let him deny himself"*, seem to confuse some. Aesthetics across the centuries have determined it to mean to deny yourself the pleasures of life. I am not at all sure of that interpretation. God has given us many things, natural things to enjoy in this life. A good cigar is one of those pleasures. Perhaps a glass of wine with your meal, or a wonderful meal where you really ate too much, but boy, was it good!. The things in life that are enjoyable are not the things Jesus meant to deny.

To put it simply, sin is what we choose sometimes. It begins, as James has shown us, in the mind and then is transferred to action. We will allow sin into our lives. In the statement in Matthew, Jesus is telling us to deny our own will and deliver ourselves to the will of God and choose not to sin. We cannot be following Jesus if we are living within the confines of our own will and never listening to the voice, the promptings or the call of the Holy Spirit. He is constantly telling us to live in His will. Don't pick that up without paying for it, don't look at that woman or man with lust in your heart, don't tell that lie again about why you were late, and don't dishonor your father or mother by disobedience or dishonor. These are all things we do to put our own will in front of what God desires for us. When we perform those kinds of acts we are choosing to deny Christ and what is right and do our own thing. We may tell Him we will be back, but right now we are choosing to do what we want to do even though we might know it is wrong. That is not self-denial, that is self-aggrandizement. Choosing to sin willfully with the intention of coming back to be forgiven later is really not a very good plan. That type of behavior is immature at best and evil at its core. We should never forget that we are following Christ and that is our main mission. And following means to take up our cross daily, whatever that may mean to you personally, and do it. Carry that cross and follow close behind Jesus. Don't go off on your own in order to satisfy some urge or temptation, but rather live in presence of God and you will be able to enjoy life's pleasures as well as be well within His will.

Counting the cost

As we begin to get closer to Jesus, we may see that this self-denial is a bit much. I have always done what I wanted and just because I now believe in Jesus, why should I have to stop what I am doing? Well, if that's your attitude, you are at a crossroads. To be a disciple of Christ you must at least attempt to cease from sin. It is imperative that all understand. You see, the attempt is why the Holy Spirit will intervene. We choose between the pleasure derived from our sin we have always enjoyed or the pleasure of overcoming that sin to enjoy God's presence as well as the many other benefits derived from being a friend, a child even, of the most powerful, yet loving and kind Being in the universe. Because that is what happens. The moment we choose God over sin, choosing to deny our self and walk toward God, angels rejoice, the Holy Spirit smiles and we are found in the presence of God. All that from making a simple choice to put our will secondary to God's will. And it is His will that we *never* sin.

The cost of discipleship is nothing. And yet, it is everything. There is no charge to follow Jesus. He is free for the taking. But it will cost you your life if you are serious about it. There will be change that happens when we come to know Jesus as our Lord and Savior. And it is the one being saved that must choose to abandon his sin and follow hard after Christ in order to make that change happen. That is why God is willing to help us, but He will never do it for us. That would make us robots. We must actively pursue change in order that it happens. And believe me, once that change begins, those in your life will notice. The ones you partied with, no longer desire to be around you because you have changed. Your family, if they are not connected to Jesus, will mock you and maybe even be angry with you. But the cost is not only in relationships, for not all will desert you because you have changed. Only those with whom you have sinned. You know, your sin-buddies.

Prepare for trouble

When you make a commitment to Christ, to embrace love instead of self-indulgence and using people for your own means, you anger your old buddy, satan. He and his demons don't like it when humans come to the knowledge of the truth, so much so that they may try to arrange trouble for you. Demonic attacks are a real thing and they always make it look like an accident. But in the spiritual world there are no coincidences. These are times when you want to be especially close to Jesus. He is your protector and your comforter and always keep in mind that He has power over all things and will bring you through whatever challenges you may face. He has said He will never leave us or forsake us. That sounds like a promise to me. That brings me great comfort. It makes me think I may not need to be broken.

CHAPTER NINE

On Being Broken

Ps 34:18

18 The LORD is near to those who have a broken heart, and saves such as have a contrite spirit.

Sometimes when we experience the most difficult things in life, we often wonder where God might be. It is difficult, to say the least, to endure some of those things that life presents. If you look around at some of the most wonderful people, you will notice that they are enduring great hardship and sometimes great suffering.

God brought me to this scripture as I wondered about the apparent inequities in life. As we go through this life, if we are paying attention, we discover that God is trying to get through to us about His plan for our lives. Each and every one of us has one of those, you know. There is no doubt in my mind that God desires each of us to serve Him in some way. Our lives are to be directed toward Him, no matter what we do for a living, no matter what our particular station in life, no matter if we are rich or poor, black, white, yellow, red or chartreuse. If you are human, God desires you, for you are a creation of His and if you awaken, you can be a child of His. Let's look at this verse in another translation, which, when I looked up the words in Hebrew, was more accurate.

It is not easy to be crushed

Ps 34:18

18 The LORD is close to the brokenhearted and saves those who are crushed in spirit. NIV

The big difference here is the phrase, "Crushed in Spirit". Contrite in spirit denotes one who is repentant, which of course we must be in order to come to the Lord, but crushed denotes one who is at the end of his rope and just cannot go on. This word in Hebrew does actually mean crushed to powder. It is an image that is hard to shake. I believe that what is meant is that in order to come to God, to make Him your Lord and let Him rule in your life, to give up your will and really begin to do His, many of us must come to this place where we are truly broken. Some of us have to hit bottom in order that we might look for a way out of the life that we tell ourselves that we enjoy. Some of us are so deep in our pride that for God to reach us, we must have everything taken from us. I know that has happened to some who may be reading this. I know that it happened to me. Now, crushing is not a pleasant thing in the physical sense. It is no more pleasant in the spiritual or emotional sense.

In fact, being crushed in the physical sense is rather easy. It's all over. But to be crushed in a spiritual sense, means that you must go on and face the next day. You must endure possibly more crushing and grinding. What David is attempting to get across to us is that we don't have to go through this crushing process. There is no *need* for us to be completely wiped out in order to come to God.

> *Ps 34:17*
> *17 The righteous cry out, and the LORD hears, and delivers them out of all their troubles.*

This does not mean that God spares those who love Him from any troubles, but rather that he brings them through those troubles. This is also proven in verse 19.

> *Ps 34:19*
> *19 Many are the afflictions of the righteous, but the LORD delivers him out of them all.*

Life is filled with disparaging things. That's life. If we never know any pain, we would never understand pleasure. God does not use these things to punish us, and I believe that for the most part, that He uses these things to teach us, because there usually is a lesson in there somewhere. Sometimes, of course, things just happen. The enemy doesn't attack us constantly, he doesn't have to. We have enough pain on our own for which he will be more than happy to take the credit. But that isn't to say that he doesn't give us some pain and attack us at times. He doesn't like it when God's people are feeling too good about God. But if we aren't keeping our eyes focused on the Lord of lights, then he doesn't even have to do anything to take our eyes off of God. So why bother? But those who are focusing on God certainly should expect the enemy to attack.

Allow your pain to lead you to God

Satan is also aware that sometimes the difficulties we go through have the affect of pushing us closer to God, rather than separating us. And that *is* what God desires for us when we encounter difficulties in our lives; that we would draw nearer to Him, that we would seek out comfort through His Spirit and that we would learn the lesson which is within each and every painful circumstance that we encounter. And there *is* a lesson in every circumstance. There is much to be learned *if* we seek to look deep into our circumstances. Sometimes that is a very big IF. When we are in the middle of difficulty, in the throes of great trouble, it is fairly tough to go searching for lessons. Most lessons are learned in hindsight. The same is true of when we are in the midst of sin and enjoying whatever it is we do, regret comes to stop and help us focus on how we can remove ourselves from this position we find ourselves in. Again, hindsight is a wonderful thing.

I think that the key is position. I am speaking of the position in which we place ourselves by our choices. We must be in the proper position. We have the availability of a great tool that enables us to be in a position of protection, both from temptation and from circumstance. The position of which I speak is our relationship with Christ. Jesus was quite descriptive in the way He showed the proper position in which we should be when we are in a relationship with Him.

Matthew 21:44
44 "And whoever falls on this stone will be broken; but on whomever it falls, it will grind him to powder."

Now, Jesus was not referring to the same crushing of which David spoke, but rather was referring to the fact that if the Rock (meaning Jesus) were to fall on someone, it would destroy him. In the context of the verse, He was referring to the Jews who were attempting to destroy Him, who denied that He was Messiah. When you look at this picture that Jesus paints here, you see a rock, a huge rock that cannot be moved, you see two positions; One on top of the Rock and one beneath it. The one who falls **on** the Rock, Jesus says will be broken. In the Greek, here, the word means exactly that; Shattered or broken.

Could this mean that anyone who comes to Christ must experience turmoil and pain? No, not at all. But it does imply that the one who falls upon the Rock will certainly be changed. The whole personality will be changed. The entire person will be different.

It can be like breaking a horse

When a horse is said to be broken, the horse is no longer the kind of horse that will buck and throw the rider and be just downright nasty. It means a kinder, gentler horse has appeared. But the same result can be obtained by using a method called "gentling" the horse. Instead of breaking it by forcing it to take a rider, a different approach is taken and the horse does not need to go through the pain of being broken. A similar thing happens to us when we have been broken on the Rock of Jesus. Now, this change can occur as a result of us coming to Christ in a gentle loving way or it may be that our stubbornness has forced us to experience a more difficult path to the Lord. If we choose the difficult path, we may certainly find that life is, at best, difficult. Without the comfort of God's guiding, we most certainly will walk down some trails that are fraught with danger and perhaps even an eternal end that will not be to our liking.

Why do we do that? Why do we put ourselves in a position that will eventually place us beneath the Rock? I think that we have this built in rebellion in our spirits and if someone tells us white, then we must see black. It's my way or the highway. I'm right and your wrong and that's all there is to that. It's called human nature and that is why over and over and over again we are admonished to overcome it. Another word for human nature is "flesh".

Flesh gets in the way

We certainly do things that are contrary to our spirit and most certainly are offensive to God. Our only way of conquering this is to deny our flesh, our human nature, both its way and its will. We are aware, or at least should be, that our humanness is opposite of our spirituality. When I say opposite, I mean that they oppose each other. They are diametrically opposed.

Paul brought this up in Romans 7.

Romans 7:22-23
22 For I delight in the law of God according to the inward man.
23 But I see another law in my members, warring against the law of my mind, and bringing me into captivity to the law of sin which is in my members.

Our flesh and our spirit are in constant battle with one another. That is why we must live in the Spirit and I don't mean our spirit but the Spirit of God. The only way that is possible is for us to completely die to the flesh and submit our will to the will of God. Wow, that just rolls off the tongue so easily. But it is not an easy thing to do. We must fall on that Rock that is Jesus and be broken. We must have a broken heart and draw near to our God.

We must fall on the Rock rather than have it fall on us. For it is in this brokenness that we become whole. Everything changes when we truly encounter this breaking of our spirit, this submission of our spirit to His. We no longer are wrestling with the flesh against the spirit, for the Spirit of God has overcome. With our submission, then we have overcome. Paul spoke of this in his second letter to the Corinthians.

2 Cor 4:7-11
7 But we have this treasure in earthen vessels, that the excellence of the power may be of God and not of us.

8 We are hard pressed on every side, yet not crushed; we are perplexed, but not in despair;
9 persecuted, but not forsaken; struck down, but not destroyed--
10 always carrying about in the body the dying of the Lord Jesus, that the life of Jesus also may be manifested in our body.
11 For we who live are always delivered to death for Jesus' sake, that the life of Jesus also may be manifested in our mortal flesh.

It is a spiritual thing

We are not able to accomplish these things in our power, in our flesh. It is only through the strength of God that we are able to conquer being hard pressed on every side, being perplexed, being persecuted and struck down. There is no winning when these things are happening to us. There is no power left in us when we have been utterly trampled by the things that life can throw at us. This is why we know that power that comes in these times is not ours, but the power of God. That is why we know that the peace that comes in these times is the peace of God and not ours… *That the excellence of the power may be of God and not us.* There is such a welcome peace when we finally discover that we no longer have to have pain and suffering in our lives, with no hope of escaping that pain and suffering, but that we can instead endure that same pain and that same suffering with joy in our hearts and the love of God showing itself at every opportunity, rather than finding it necessary to talk about our pain constantly, or to dwell on it, we talk about what God has done for us and what we see Him do for others. The power of God shines forth like a light with the brilliance of a thousand suns.

We really do not do much good

The good things we have done, we realize are not the things we have done, but rather the things that God has done. But take heart, this is no mean feat. It is not a small thing to be used by God, even in small ways. There is no little thing done for someone in need. Jesus mentioned a cup of cold water. That cup of water certainly isn't a big deal to the one giving it, but if it is done in the right spirit, not saying, "let me give you this", but rather, "I give you this in the name of Jesus" then the person receiving it will receive double blessing. They are not only refreshed by the water, but they see how you have given your life to Christ. It must never be us who does the work, but we must come to the point where we realize that we are merely the tools being used in the hands of Christ. Not our strength, not our power, not even our idea. The word "I" must be eliminated from our vocabulary in order that the name of Christ be lifted up. Dare we elevate ourselves to the same level as Him by claiming that what He has done, He could not have done without me?

This is part of the brokenness, the positioning that allows Christ to become more of us and **us** to become less of us and more of Him. When we fall upon the Rock and become broken, we discover that God truly desires to give us those aspects of His personality that will enable us to give away what we possess, and I'm not speaking of physical things here. Without those attributes of God in our lives, and I mean reigning in our lives, we are unable to truly say, "In the name of Jesus". We can only do things in our own name. "Look what I did. I did a godly thing, isn't that neat?" Whenever we do anything in the name of God and then point to ourselves as the one doing it, we actually take away from the thing that was done, as well as the one who really did it. We rip Jesus off. There is nothing wrong with being recognized as the instrument that God has used for something, but if you do something, even a godly thing, and then mention it to everyone you meet, you are stealing from Jesus.

Give God the Glory

It would be better to claim what God has done in your life, how He has taken you from that to this. The miracles He has done, both for you and around you. Look around! God is not sleeping. Pay attention. Every single day there are things being done by the Lord that are truly amazing. Give Him glory for those things. As I said, it may be something small, but without a doubt God has given you or done something for you this week or inspired you to do something for someone else.

Volunteer for being broken. Submit to His will. Challenge yourself each day with drawing nearer to Him, and then most importantly, look within yourself and see where you are. Check your position on the Rock. Are you being broken on top of it or are you being crushed beneath it? To be crushed is to deny Him; Denying His power, denying His authority, denying His love and denying His ability to bring you to a place on top of the rock.

Don't be in that position of denial, but rather acceptance of God's will for you and in the position of performing that will for the simple reason that it will make you more and draw you nearer than ever before to His love.

We have examples

Have you ever stopped to think that the great men and women of the bible were not always great, not always strong, and in fact there were times in their lives when some of them were some of the most miserable excuses for humans that ever walked the face of the earth and other times when they did not realize that God was near to them. In each one of these people, by going back in the history of their lives, we will discover someone who was either out for their own gain, or trusted in their own resources, or pride took hold of them and very nearly ended their usefulness to God.

There is one common thread that unites each person who has ever come to the Lord and that includes those to whom we look to as biblical heroes as well as you and me and also signifies each one who ever will come to Him and it seems that the deeper this particular event drives into the soul of each person, the greater their devotion is to God. And so we see why each of the greatest bible personalities had to experience this in their lives to a most extraordinary degree.

Brokenness is necessary

I'm speaking of being broken by God. Now this brokenness is different for each of us and just as I can't tell you how you should like your eggs, or what color should be your favorite, I can't tell you how you should be broken. Paul was broken on the road to Damascus when Jesus confronted him and he was made blind. Being blinded should be enough to break someone, but being healed from that same blindness was probably the capper for Paul. For just as all who refused to see Christ in His great light either have been or will be blinded by that light, many have come to Him as a result of that great light.

David was broken after his sin with Bathsheba. It took a great sin, adultery compounded with murder and then an attempt to hide it to break a man after God's own heart. But once David was confronted by Nathan the prophet and he finally realized that he couldn't hide his sin from God, David was broken and able to be once more used by God in mighty ways. But it took the death of his son to accomplish that.

And that is something of which we must take note. If we refuse to be broken, if we fight back in anger against the power of God to try to change us and shape us, we will still endure the pain that is always associated with brokenness, but we may never come out of the place where we were brought to be broken. For example, what if David had never accepted God's judgment concerning Bathsheba? What if after the experience of losing his son that was born from an adulterous relationship he still attempted to hide his sin from the people of Israel and even refused to acknowledge to himself that it was sin at all? What if he would have said to himself, "Self, I have a great relationship here and Bathsheba, she's sure a great gal. I only did what I had to do to make sure we got to spend the rest of our lives together."

If David had taken that attitude and literally refused to acknowledge his sin and repent and accept the consequences of his actions, he would have floundered for years and surely lost his standing as a man after God's own heart. Plus he would have lived in pain and confusion for the rest of his days, for if we refuse to look into the face of our sin and confront it, we surely can never repent from it. But he didn't. He needed someone (Nathan) to show him the darkness of his sin, but then he did the right thing. He asked for mercy and repented. Read Psalm 51 sometime to gain understanding of David's heart toward God and the sin he committed.

You must stand against your sin

The same is true of addicts and alcoholics. If they refuse to see that there is a problem with their drug or alcohol use, they will forever be imprisoned by the very thing they refuse to acknowledge. If you can't see your enemy, or at least the results of his work, you can certainly not defeat him. That's why David **was** a man after God's own heart. He did confront his sin after it was brought to him by Nathan. He had been hiding up to that point, from what, I'm not sure. But guilt makes us do some very strange things indeed, mostly cower in fear.

In order to truly understand brokenness, we must first discover that the result of being broken by God will always be a spiritual reward, a spiritual renewal. If you seek the things of this world, then I suggest you go invest in the stock market or some other money making venture. God is not interested in your physical and financial well being nearly as much as your spiritual growth. And if you ever find that your financial or physical or worldly needs are in any way compromising your spiritual health, and you belong to God, prepare for a really rough ride. The only thing we own that will go when we leave this life is our spirit. Unless we come to that knowledge, we live apart from God. When we realize that, we begin to chase God and when we begin to chase after Him we begin that process of becoming broken. And that's just one of the reasons we must count the cost. Now understand that being broken doesn't have to be God taking everything you own; your family, all your relationships, your home, your clothes, all your money and your dog and your cat and leaving you with only a bowl for begging and penniless on the street...necessarily. Then again, maybe that's what it will take for you to get it. Some of us are pretty stubborn, while others seem to understand and come to Him and bend to His will without those extreme measures being necessary. Try to be in that category.

Jacob was an example

This whole subject is best explained by what occurred in the life of Jacob. Jacob, through trickery, had wrested the birthright of his brother Esau from him. This left a rift between the brothers that lasted many years. When Jacob was finally convinced that he needed to repair this breach in their brotherhood, he went to Esau, but not alone. (Genesis 32) He took the whole family, servants, goats, cattle etc. When he got close to where Esau was he broke the whole party down into several different groups and sent them on one at a time. He told them that as they encountered Esau, to tell him that all this was a gift from Jacob. He sent everyone ahead and stayed alone on the bank of the river. This is where he wrestled with someone all night until dawn. Jacob was being broken during this wrestling match. He struggled and fought with God and all the time didn't even know why he was struggling. Sound familiar?

Eventually, God touched his hip joint and put it out of place….for the rest of his life. But Jacob was a changed man after this event. He wasn't the conniving reckless schemer he was before and it was at this time that God changed his name to Israel. He walked with a crutch for the rest of his life, but that was indicative of the fact that he would forever need to depend on God for all he had. Jacob was changed.

When we encounter God, it is quite normal for us to argue with Him, to struggle with Him to deny His power, to deny His provision, and to continue to desire to do things the way we've always done them. When that happens we become Jacob wrestling with God on the bank of the river attempting to overcome the one who desires nothing more than to provide for us and show us a better way.

It's really easy to look at the story of Jacob and say, "Boy, I sure wouldn't have wrestled with that angel all night long. I would have figured it out right away." Or maybe, "Boy those disciples were sure dumb, they had Jesus right next to them and they couldn't figure out that He was Messiah." Yet we have events in our lives or in the lives of someone near to us or perhaps even things we hear about in passing that show us the power of God and the miraculous ways He provides and does things for people and we continue to deny His power in our own lives. Hindsight is always 20/20.

But God rewards foresight. God rewards faith. One of the reasons God considered Abraham as a righteous man was because of his faith, his belief in what had yet to come. God had said it and Abraham believed it. Paul also saw and understood this as part of the way in which God interacts with man because he explained Abraham's faith like this:

> *Romans 4:19-21 19 And not being weak in faith, he did not consider his own body, already dead (since he was about a hundred years old), and the deadness of Sarah's womb.*
> *20 He did not waver at the promise of God through unbelief, but was strengthened in faith, giving glory to God,*
> *21 and being fully convinced that what He had promised He was also able to perform.*

If God told me at a hundred years old that my wife who was ninety years was going to give birth, I'm not so sure I could say, "Yes Lord, that's fine." But we must ask ourselves this question; If God told me *anything*, would I believe it? We should all ask ourselves this question: Is God telling me something right now?

How do we hear God?

Many of us live in a state of ignoring God because He doesn't come to us through the television or radio. We would believe a stranger on TV that tells us that his product will make our whites whiter and our colors brighter, but when God speaks to us through His word or a dream or through a word of knowledge given by someone, we usually find it difficult to believe. We must see that He sometimes comes to us through other people and places we don't really expect. When Abraham encountered God just prior to the destruction of Sodom and Gomorrah, (Genesis. 19) he was sitting in the door of his tent when three men walked by. One of them was God. Abraham was just sitting there enjoying a peaceful sit, and all of a sudden, God showed up. He reiterated the promise that soon he would have a son. Abraham believed Him. He didn't wrestle with Him, he didn't argue with Him, he didn't need to be broken by Him. He believed God.

How much better for us when we do not feel the need to wrestle with God and ultimately be broken in order to discover that He was right all along? As we struggle against Him we will discover that we will indeed ultimately lose. And denying His power to do anything is struggling with Him. Listen to what Solomon said in:

> *Proverbs 3:5-6*
> *5 Trust in the LORD with all your heart, and lean not on your own understanding;*
> *6 In all your ways acknowledge Him, and He shall direct your paths.*

It is when we lean on our own understanding of things that we wrestle with God. Then we will become broken. It is when we fight His will, his leading in our life and insist on our own way of doing things, that God will find it necessary to show us a better way. If that's what it takes for God to get our attention, then He will do it.

Strength comes from that brokenness because when we learn that in our brokenness, we have drawn nearer to His strength, the learning portion of our test is done. It is then when true Peace arrives. And what an awesome peace it is. Paul described it in:

> *Phil 4:6-7*
> *6 Be anxious for nothing, but in everything by prayer and supplication,*
> *with thanksgiving, let your requests be made known to God;*
> *7 and the peace of God, which surpasses all understanding, will guard*
> *your hearts and minds through Christ Jesus.*

We need be anxious for nothing because the God of the universe is, believe it or not, in control. If we trust Him, then trust Him. If we believe Him, then believe Him. God does nothing out of selfishness, but only out of love. He never breaks us to destroy us but rather to strengthen us. Exercise your muscles and your body will grow strong, exercise your knowledge and your mind will grow strong, exercise your faith and your spirit will grow strong.

CHAPTER TEN

Scars

2 Timothy 2:3-4

3 You therefore must endure hardship as a good soldier of Jesus Christ.
4 No one engaged in warfare entangles himself with the affairs of this
life, that he may please him who enlisted him as a soldier.

In most Christian circles, much ado is made about scars. But the scars of which people speak are either the scars of Jesus or the scars we have received in our lives, the ones that shape us and make us into who we are. *They* come from all sorts of weapons, like whips and knives and guns and dogs and cats not to mention the emotional and psychological scars and the scars left on our souls and minds from sin and abuse and hatred as well as all sorts of various other reasons.

You see, that's what happens in a war. You get some scars and you leave some scars. But in a war, if you're a good warrior, you leave more scars than you get and the reason for that is that you become proficient with your weapons. And as Christians what is most important is that we leave scars on our enemy rather than bragging about the scars we have received.

Now Jesus did not leave us unprepared to be soldiers in this war. But there are some things we must realize if we are to be prepared for battle. These two verses are to remind us that we are engaged in war and that we must always be prepared for two things in order to fight and become a good soldier. First if we are soldiers, there will be hardship. Get over it. We enlisted. No one who belongs to Christ was drafted. We choose the life we choose. Secondly, if we are soldiers in this army, there is no taking a day off, an hour off or even a minute off. We are on duty all the time. And that is so very difficult to do. You see, our enemy is always looking for a way to get to us. If we become engaged in activities that keep us from being aware of who we are, where we are, and who our enemy is, then we put ourselves at risk of obtaining a wound in the battle.

Do your job

Imagine a guard who was not actually guarding, or someone in battle who was not actually fighting in the battle, but just ignoring all that was happening around him. He or she puts not only themselves in jeopardy, but their fellow soldiers as well. For whether or not we realize it, we are in a continuous battle. Our enemy surely does realize that. And the thing about him is that he is very patient and willing to wait for the right opportunity to strike. He has only to see that we are in a vulnerable position and BOOM, he is there to show us something that will take us away from the presence of God. It may be exciting, it may be vile, and we may fight it, and we may not...but if we succumb to it, we probably will again and again until one day it will leave a very nasty scar on us. It will break through our defenses and we will soon choose it over God because of what it does for us. And then we are prisoners in a place we definitely don't want to be, and discovering that we had the key, but threw it away.

But we need not fight this battle in this way. We don't have to be defeated and destroyed, locked in a cell with no key and that is simply because this battle has already been fought …..and won. You see we have the victory on the battlefield and it was Christ who won it for us, but we can turn that victory over to our enemy so easily by not using the tools, the weapons He gave us in order that we might continue to live in that victory. These are things we have all heard of before and I want to quickly mention them here. They're found in:

> *Eph 6:14-17*
> *14 Stand therefore, having girded your waist with truth, having put on*
> *the breastplate of righteousness,*
> *15 and having shod your feet with the preparation of the gospel of peace;*
> *16 above all, taking the shield of faith with which you will be able to*
> *quench all the fiery darts of the wicked one.*
> *17 And take the helmet of salvation, and the sword of the Spirit, which*
> *is the word of God;*

If we were not supposed to be ready for war, do you think that Paul would have needed to write these verses? You don't need weapons or armor for peacetime. You see we have here a lot of defensive weapons. Our waist is protected our breast area (our heart), our feet and of course we have a shield. Defensive weapons are meant to keep us from getting scars. But there is one offensive weapon in this collection and it is meant to make scars. The sword of the Spirit, the Word of God is what we must use if we want to inflict some pain on our enemy, and let's face it, it would be good to beat up on him for once wouldn't it?

Fear paralyzes us

We are sometimes in fear of what the enemy wants to do to us and we seem to keep that sword behind our back when it should be out in front of us and we should be swinging away. Now of course I'm speaking of spiritual enemies, spiritual scars and spiritual weapons. They are the things of God. Our enemy is not one we can see or touch, but we can see the results of his presence and we can touch what evil he brings before us to take us from the presence of God.

There are two verses we should examine to understand our enemy. We have all heard them before, but it's sometimes good to be reminded of those things we face, especially when we cannot see them.

The first is:

> *Eph 6:12*
> *12 For we do not wrestle against flesh and blood, but against principalities, against powers, against the rulers of the darkness of this age, against spiritual hosts of wickedness in the heavenly places.*

We must always keep in the front of our minds that our enemy is one we cannot see. We can see the results of his handiwork, but we cannot see him…..or them. ***They are the rulers of the darkness of this age***…..and that is a thought that should keep you on your toes. They are the commanders of wickedness and they strive to keep you from God.

The second verse is:

> 1 Pet 5:8
> *8 Be sober, be vigilant; because your adversary the devil walks about like a roaring lion, seeking whom he may devour.*

Our enemy is always ready, always waiting to exploit your weaknesses, your fears, your difficulties and he hides and makes you think that you have everything under control. He remains hidden until you have chosen a moment to relax your defenses and suddenly he springs, he attacks, his desire is to destroy you and/or everything you love, your relationship with God, your happiness, your peace. The results of which look something like weeping and sadness and pain, and I am speaking of both spiritually and physically.

God has provided us with a great weapon

So the point is, what can we do as Christians to destroy that enemy, to defeat him, to make scars on him rather than be on the receiving end all the time? We have the greatest weapon in the universe at our disposal and it isn't an axe, or a gun or even a tank. He is a spiritual weapon and He comes from the One Who has made all things and we often portray Him as a dove, but He is the Holy Spirit of God and He has great power and He is there to help us in both our relationship with God and in overcoming the one who would destroy that relationship.

Jesus said:

John 14:16-17
16 "And I will pray the Father, and He will give you another Helper, that He may abide with you forever--
*17 "the Spirit of truth, whom the world cannot receive, because it neither sees Him nor knows Him; but you know Him, for He dwells **with you** and will be **in you**.*

I can't think of a weapon that could be better than one that is not only with us, but in us. How can this be? When it comes down to it, it doesn't matter how it can be, just know that it is something promised by Jesus and God keeps his promises. In Isaiah 55, God states that His ways are not our ways and His thoughts are not our thoughts and that His ways are beyond our understanding. I'm pretty sure that's true. So what does that mean for us in our everyday life? Just everything!

Suffering sometimes happens

If we find ourselves in the midst of something, whether it be a temptation, or a trial, or a need or some difficulty.....anything the enemy has arranged, God is able to overcome it and bring us through it. The way we are able to utilize the power of God is to discover His will for our lives in the situation we now face, whatever that situation may be. If we are living in the Spirit, walking in the Spirit, listening for the Spirit, we are able to discern what God desires us to do. But if we don't even consult God when things come up, how will we ever know what it is He desires for us? Consulting Him is easy....we get on our knees, and we ask Him to reveal to us His will for us. Even Jesus did so and we must always remember that Jesus asked that He wouldn't have to go through what He was about to go through, but the answer was no, because sometimes the answer *is* no.

Sometimes the answer is, "You must go through this trial." But you will be better because of it, you will leave scars on the enemy because of it, you will draw nearer to God because of it. Can you imagine where we would be if Jesus had stood up in the garden and said, "Well, it may be Your will that I have to do this, but since it's me, and I'm going to be the one who is actually doing it, thanks but no thanks."

We would all be lost because of a lack of will on His part to do His Father's will. But because of His willingness to perform the Father's will, we have the right to enter into His kingdom. He is able to strengthen us to also do the Father's will, whatever that will may be and he is able to protect us within that same will. We must come to the conclusion, eventually, that His will is going to be accomplished with or without us, so we might as well get on board right away. He is able to preserve us for we are never alone when we walk in His will.

Inflicting scars on the enemy

Do you want to leave a scar on your enemy? Then there is only one way. We must reach out to Christ in all we do, for He is reaching out to us. We must be seeking His will in all we do, not acting on our own, for if we walk away from His will we walk into an unknown place, and it may be a place of grave danger, a desert, a place that will be almost certainly worse than the place we may now be, even though we may be in a scary place now.

Do you want to leave some scars on your enemy? Then live a life of holiness. Love God with all your heart, and love your neighbor as yourself. Think of others before yourself. Visit a nursing home and show them some of God's love by talking with residents or playing a game with them, feed some hungry people, or even volunteer with meals on wheels in your community. Start up a program in your church that does something for those in need of anything. Find something you can do to assist the marginalized in your community. These are all things that show the love of God to those in need of that love. And trust me, most don't know they even need it, but they may discover the depth of the love of God because of your kindness toward them.

Do you want to leave some scars on your enemy? Pray, and then pray, and then pray some more. Pray without ceasing. Give no quarter to your enemy and you will defeat him. Chase after God with every waking moment. Don't get involved in anything that takes you from his presence….anything! If people at work or just nearby are cursing or telling dirty jokes, don't be afraid to either walk away or even tell them you find that offensive. Stand up for what is right at every opportunity. Trust God to do what He said He would do and then learn what this means:

> *Eph 3:20-21*
> *20 Now to Him who is able to do exceedingly abundantly above all that we ask or think, according to the power that works in us,*
> *21 to Him be glory in the church by Christ Jesus to all generations, forever and ever. Amen.*

The power that works within us has already given us the victory, but we must learn to live within that victory, not cowering before our enemy, or sometimes returning to him for temporary satisfaction. He is already defeated by the shed blood of Jesus. Give him nothing but disappointment at never having the satisfaction of seeing us leave the altar of the living God. Leave him with only scars and memories of what we once were and the realization that we are now new creatures in Christ. This will leave a permanent scar on him and it will spoil his plans for your future. You will be filled with a great sense of accomplishment and joy as you stand over him and look to heaven for your reward.

The importance of prayer

I cannot overstate the importance of prayer in any attempt to overcome some stubborn sin that has you trapped in its grip. Jesus was pretty adamant about how we are to approach knowledge of God.

> *Matt 7:7-8*
> *"Ask, and it will be given to you; seek, and you will find; knock, and it will be opened to you.*
> *8 For everyone who asks receives, and he who seeks finds, and to him who knocks it will be opened.*

The knowledge we are given when we seek is invaluable in learning to overcome our sin. But we must seek this knowledge. It may come after much pleading, much introspection, many hours of emotional ups and downs. This is because in prayer we will find ourselves wrestling with God and our own flesh. We may seem caught in the middle of a battle between our flesh and our spirit. The only way to win this battle is through sincere contact with the Holy Spirit of God.

The prayer for deliverance from any sin that has held you for a long time is one that must be delivered from the heart of a transformed mind. It cries out for deliverance as it feels trapped by the lust that holds your soul in this dark place. This may be the most important prayer someone in this situation ever prays. There will be weeping, for your sin has overwhelmed you and your very soul is in pain. Your desire to be set free must be declared aloud to the Lord and the wrestling will begin. This match may go on for years, but if you are sincere in prayer and you have learned repentance, then the victory will be yours.

138

CHAPTER ELEVEN

Strongholds

2 Corinthinas 5:17
Therefore, if anyone is in Christ, he is a new creation; old things have passed away; behold, all things have become new.

When we come to Christ, we are told that some pretty amazing things happen. The most amazing of these things (at least to me) is that the old things are passed away and all things are made new. We become a brand new creation. If you really think about that, it is a truly incredible thing. And most of us, when we first come to the Lord, experience a truly wonderful change in our lives. It is a most incredible experience. But after a number of years, or after a few difficult things, many Christians tend to draw away from the passion they once had at the beginning of their Christian experience and begin to look more and more like the world they left. Even King David cried out to the Lord in Psalm 51 to restore unto him the joy of his salvation. If David can lose that joy due to sin, what makes any of us think we can't as well?

Christians should not be worldly

It is an impossible thing for a Christian to look just like the world. We are commanded by Christ to come out of the world and be apart, yet when we look around at the church, it is often difficult to tell the difference between the world and the church. This just should not be. So we must ask ourselves why. Why is it that so many Christians look so much like they did before they came to Christ? I believe that most often an affiliation with the world is due to some stronghold in our life. These can manifest themselves in a physical way, but make no mistake these are spiritual strongholds and they keep us from a close relationship with Christ.

> *2 Cor 10:3-6*
> *3 For though we walk in the flesh, we do not war according to the flesh.*
> *4 For the weapons of our warfare are not carnal but mighty in God for pulling down strongholds,*
> *5 casting down arguments and every high thing that exalts itself against the knowledge of God, bringing every thought into captivity to the obedience of Christ,*
> *6 and being ready to punish all disobedience when your obedience is fulfilled.*

Strongholds are things that keep us in a place other than in the presence of God. They can make us long for His presence in our lives, while at the same time remove us to a place of worldly and physical control rather than taking us in a spiritual direction. Strongholds have a way of making you think you are in a good place where no harm can come to you, while you are in a place of extreme danger. And this danger is only due to the absence of God in your life.

These verses say that the weapons we have are mighty in God for pulling down strongholds. Funny thing about weapons though, unless you pick them up and use them, they do absolutely no good. The strongholds that can do the most damage to our spirits are pride, rebellion, idolatry, fear, insecurity, control, desire and bitterness. These things can make us cower like children in front of a mad dog if we are not delivered and that is simply because we refuse to admit that we live in one or more of these strongholds. I will attempt to address each one of these individually.

Addressing Pride

Pride is probably the most difficult to see in ourselves simply because of its very nature. Pride consumes us with the inability to seek anything but our own good, our own counsel, and our own achievements. When others are speaking we are ignoring them because we know that what they have to say is not important.

But most importantly of all, pride prevents God from doing any work within us simply because it holds shut the door that allows humility to open *that same* door. Unless we overcome pride and humble ourselves and come towards God, we *cannot* truly come to God. Humility is the first step toward a relationship with Him and it is something that God honors above all else. I think this is so because even though Jesus is the creator of all things, He humbled Himself and came to earth and went to the cross in order to open the door to the Kingdom of God for us.

Pride was the first sin when Lucifer rebelled against God. So many sins evolve from pride that is difficult to name them all. In fact all strongholds including the following have a basis in pride, so it might be argued that pride is the mother of all sins.

The Stronghold of Rebellion

Rebellion is something that is found in many, if not most, humans. It is closely associated with pride and remains a detriment to any relationship with God. Rebellion usually says, *"I know better than you, so why should I do what you tell me?"* We become like a child that refuses to obey a parent when the parent tells them to stay out of the street, only to run out into the street, be hit by a car and killed. The parent was trying to protect the child, but the child thought the parent didn't know what he was talking about. They both paid for the child's rebellion. When God gives us instruction, it isn't for His benefit, it's for ours. The author of Hebrews addressed this in:

> *Heb 3:14-15*
> *14 For we have become partakers of Christ if we hold the beginning of*
> *our confidence steadfast to the end,*
> *15 while it is said: "Today, if you will hear His voice, Do not harden*
> *your hearts as in the rebellion."*

This is a quote from Psalm 95. The rebellion to which the Psalm refers is the rebellion of the Israelites in the desert. It caused many to perish. But our rebellion can cause us to deny His sovereignty and ignore His warnings only to find out in the end that He was right. We miss out on the many blessings He desires to give us and it may be that our entire life is spent in the valley when it could have been on the mountain top of His revelation for our life. Having God revealed in us is indeed the place where He wants us to be, but that can't happen if we are living a life of rebellion and insisting on everything "our" way.

What's an idol?

Idolatry is indeed a difficult place to find oneself. That is due to the fact that it is the most difficult to identify in ourselves. When we hear the word, it conjures up visions of bowing down before a stone or graven image, but it goes oh, so much deeper than that.

> *Ps 135:14-15*
> *14 For the LORD will judge His people, and He will have compassion on His servants.*
> *15 **The idols of the nations are silver and gold, the work of men's hands.***

This sounds as though idols are mostly money and I could even see that it could be interpreted as someone's work but the fact is, idolatry can be anything to which we devote an excessive amount of time and/or treasure and replaces God in our life. When we spend an inordinate amount of time with sports, money, television, chasing the opposite sex, books, work, play and a host of other things, we are participating in idolatry. The problem is that when we are engaged in any of these things, it usually doesn't seem as though it is an inordinate amount of time, especially work. That's because many people see their work as an absolutely important place that cannot be handled with less than a twelve hour day. But half your life devoted to anything can certainly become idolatry.

And even less time spent with something can be considered idolatry if it is a struggle to pull yourself away when God calls you to something with Him. If God isn't first, then that just might be an indication that there may be a problem. Idolatry is a lust for that which is not God and the only way it can be defeated is a conscious effort to draw near to Him and stay near to Him. It isn't easy, but it will make your life one of knowing that God will sincerely give all to you. We must learn to give priority to those pursuits which are godly.

The danger of owning fear

Fear is another difficult stronghold from which we should all break free. Fear is ingrained in our humanity as a protective device but can easily overtake us if we allow it. Our greatest fears are those things unknown. That stands to reason...sort of. We have an iceberg mentality, or all that we see above the water is OK, I can steer around it, but what lies beneath? Is it something that can hurt me, destroy me, or cause me pain? The greatest detriment to a Christian life as a result of fear is the fact that fear will prevent you from utilizing the great gifts which God has given you. It may paralyze you in a fear of failure or rejection. When Paul wrote to Timothy he reminded him of this fact:

> *2 Tim 1:6-9*
> *6 Therefore I remind you to stir up the gift of God which is in you through the laying on of my hands.*
> *7 For God has not given us a spirit of fear, but of power and of love and of a sound mind.*
> *8 Therefore do not be ashamed of the testimony of our Lord, nor of me His prisoner, but share with me in the sufferings for the gospel according to the power of God,*
> *9 who has saved us and called us with a holy calling, not according to our works, but according to His own purpose and grace which was given to us in Christ Jesus before time began,*

Fear is a tool of the enemy used to keep us in a place of bondage. I don't know how many addicts I've known who are afraid to leave their present lifestyle because it has become so comfortable. They're used to it and are afraid to go somewhere else simply because it is unknown and they think they do not have the strength to face it without their drug or drink. Smokers are the same way. That first step of really seriously quitting any particular sin or habit creates the same fear and can be very difficult indeed. You must overcome your fear of living without a cigarette or any sin.

Once a person can do that, they are halfway home. We must come to the knowledge that if we have placed our lives in the hands of God, we must learn to trust His guidance, and His plan for our lives.

The hopelessness of insecurity

Insecurity can bring us to a place of depression and sadness on an almost daily basis. It is akin to fear because it does not believe. Insecurity is the manifestation of defeat in a life that has not known victory and it may even be so closely related to fear that it becomes fearful of victory. It is the opposite of hope and therefore cannot be found in God and should not be found in His people. All of God's promises are meant to give us hope. They are meant for us to trust in the One who made those promises that He will bring us to a place of rest. Faith in His promises, faith that He is able to accomplish what He has promised should be enough to inspire confidence in us. If it isn't we are lost anyway and we can be secure in that. Confidence is knowing that God is with you in all that you do. If that doesn't bring you confidence, nothing will.

Do you need control?

Control is a very dangerous thing. Once again, we find that it is akin to pride and may cause us to ignore or perhaps not even listen to what God or even other people may be trying to tell us. And it could be for many different reasons. But it always comes down to the fact that we think we know better than anyone, including God, (even though we would never verbalize that) what exactly should be done in all situations. Being a Pastor, I know that Pastors are the worst at this particular stronghold, as well as others who live or have lived in management positions. Refusing to hand over control is a handicap to seeking God's wisdom and knowledge. When we fail to seek Him, we will most certainly fail to submit to Him. And if we fail to submit to His leading we are bound to make some really bad decisions somewhere.

Misplaced desires

Desire we have spoken of before in this book. Hope creates desire in us and desire creates hope and as long as that desire is placed in Christ, there is no problem, but once desire is attuned to worldly pleasures, especially sexual matters, desire can lead to a plethora of darkness and evil. James had the best explanation of how desires can rule our hearts.

James 1:14-15
14 But each one is tempted when he is drawn away by his own desires and enticed.
15 Then, when desire has conceived, it gives birth to sin; and sin, when it is full-grown, brings forth death.

Desire is necessary to our completeness, or our wholeness, for without it there could be no hope. We need desire to live a fulfilled life. Knowing that, the enemy uses our desire to tempt us with worldly things. And when I say worldly, I mean anything that will take us from the presence of God because it is sin. Not all things of the world are sin, just as all things spiritual are not of God. Remember that satan is a spirit as well. Our imaginations are a good thing because they have allowed the visions created there to bring forth some wonderful inventions that have made life better for billions of people but misplaced desires have ruined many people. Be very careful how you control your desires.

Dangerous Bitterness

Of all the strongholds, the most difficult one to break is the stronghold of bitterness. When we form in our hearts a feeling of disdain for someone or something, we can develop a heart that is poisoned by the lack of mercy and forgiveness that grows. The very word bitterness in Greek means an acrid flavor, especially poison.

Heb 12:14-15
14 Pursue peace with all people, and holiness, without which no one will see the Lord:

15 looking diligently lest anyone fall short of the grace of God; lest any root of bitterness springing up cause trouble, and by this many become defiled;

When we become bitter, God has a very difficult time getting His light into that darkness because those who live with a bitter heart seem to revel in it. They may plan their schedules and words to cause pain for that which they hold this disdain. It is darkness indeed. In fact all of these things of which we have been speaking have an element of darkness which, released to grow in their own merit will snuff out God's light completely simply because to embrace any of these things is to turn our backs on the values of God.

Are we rejecting God?

When we curl up comfortably within any of these eight strongholds we look just like the world. When we embrace pride, rebellion, idolatry, fear, insecurity, control, misplaced desires or bitterness we show God that we reject His love, joy, peace, patience, kindness, goodness, faithfulness, gentleness and self-control. And we certainly do not reveal His grace. The only way to remove ourselves from these strongholds is to turn ourselves to the revelation of the light of God, to the knowledge found in God's Word and to the peace discovered in His presence.

When we seek comfort in the world, we will receive the comfort of the world, which is temporary, and very destructive to our spirits. When we seek God, we have been *promised* that we will find Him, a loving generous Father who has only our best intentions in mind Who will grant us comfort during any storm, peace during any turmoil.

The way to destroy the stronghold(s) in our lives that are worldly is to build for ourselves new places of rest, new strongholds built upon the Rock of Jesus Christ. They are discovered, one book, one chapter, one verse, even one word at a time in the places where God has breathed His breath of life; in His word. I have not published here a comprehensive list of strongholds, but rather a list of some of the most common in mankind. We are each unique in how we approach God as well as how we receive Him.

146

There are many strongholds not mentioned at all, but if you have some stronghold in your life which takes you from the presence of God, even for a moment, and leads you into sin, then, please, with all haste, rid yourself of that stronghold. Ask God to take it from you and release you from its grip. Unless we seek Him, we will not find Him. Let Him ignite, or reignite that flame within your heart, let it begin today.

CHAPTER TWELVE

All you need is love

I began this book by saying that anything done outside the scope of love is sin. It is true. Love is the song of the innocent, the redeemed, and the ones who own the mind of Christ. This love has nothing to do with physical love, but spiritual love for the life before it. That is the love described in 1Corinthians 13. It comes from the heart, not the body. It reacts with action rather than simply watching and the reaction is usually in the form of compassion.

When I look around the world I surely do not see much of that kind of love. We could use Mother Teresa as an example. When she looked at the lepers, the ones who had stumps where arms and legs once were, Those rejected by society, the beaten and nearly destroyed, she didn't look away. Her arms reached for them to give comfort and a bit of joy to those whose lives were so difficult. This is a spiritual sensing that overwhelms the physical in a manner not yet understood by mankind. It is a spiritual sense. It is the mind of Christ. Paul described this in his first letter to the Corinthian church.

1 Cor 2:13-16

13 These things we also speak, not in words which man's wisdom teaches but which the Holy Spirit teaches, comparing spiritual things with spiritual.

14 But the natural man does not receive the things of the Spirit of God, for they are foolishness to him; nor can he know them, because they are spiritually discerned.

15 But he who is spiritual judges all things, yet he himself is rightly judged by no one.

16 For "who has known the mind of the Lord that he may instruct Him?" But we have the mind of Christ.

The mind of Christ is the mind that is directed by the Holy Spirit. It has submitted all to Him and takes his direction from Him. It is not possible to show true agape love without first owning the mind of Christ. So you can see why anything not done in love is sin. Love never sins and we cannot sin when Christ is in control.

We must look through God's eyes

Christ-like love is the state of seeing all through God's merciful eyes. That includes showing mercy to those who may not deserve it. Even the darkness can be forgiven if it does two things; Submits to God by asking for forgiveness and repents from its darkness. That's why Jesus has instructed us to act in the same manner. Forgiveness of those who sin against us is mandated by order of Jesus. We are to be light. The nature of sin is dark and the nature of God is light. Light is much more powerful as anyone who has ever pulled back blackout curtains in a dark room in the middle of the day may understand. (You may have to live in Alaska to understand this example) Light instantly invades the room and overcomes the darkness. I've always thought God made that happen as a teaching tool for us. We are to be light and overcome the darkness.

It isn't always easy to love. Let's examine that; Homeless people are yucky, I don't want to touch them. Sick people are, uh, sick. Who wants to be around that? People in jail are criminals. No one would desire to be in a place where criminals are locked up, yet, these are the ones we are instructed to love. I want to examine the scripture that gives us God's view of love;

Matt 25:31-40
31 "When the Son of Man comes in His glory, and all the holy angels
with Him, then He will sit on the throne of His glory.
32 All the nations will be gathered before Him, and He will separate
them one from another, as a shepherd divides his sheep from the goats.
33 And He will set the sheep on His right hand, but the goats on the left.
34 Then the King will say to those on His right hand, 'Come, you blessed
of My Father, inherit the kingdom prepared for you from the foundation
of the world:

35 for I was hungry and you gave Me food; I was thirsty and you gave Me drink; I was a stranger and you took Me in;
36 I was naked and you clothed Me; I was sick and you visited Me; I was in prison and you came to Me.'
37 "Then the righteous will answer Him, saying, 'Lord, when did we see You hungry and feed You, or thirsty and give You drink?
38 When did we see You a stranger and take You in, or naked and clothe You?
39 Or when did we see You sick, or in prison, and come to You?'
40 And the King will answer and say to them, 'Assuredly, I say to you, inasmuch as you did it to one of the least of these My brethren, you did it to Me.'

After this we should be able to understand the mind of Christ. It loves those who are hungry, homeless, naked, sick and in prison. That prison can be the prison of sin. We need to help those whom we see struggling in all ways and even those in sin. And remember, if sin is anything not done in love, then we are asked to love the sinner as well. We must show them the way out of their sin, just as we show the homeless a way out or homelessness or the hungry a way out of starvation.

Can we love from afar?

Love requires action. We can love from afar in some ways but sometimes we must get up close and personal. It may be that you are supporting and contributing to ministries that do all these things. They feed the hungry and supply clothes to the naked; they visit the sick and those in prison as well as take in homeless and many other acts of kindness. But let me ask you a question; When you send off your gift to the ministry you are supporting, do you pray over it? Do you ask God to place it where it will do the most good? Do you vet the agencies to which you contribute to make sure all your money isn't used for administrative costs? Having worked for more than twenty years in the non-profit world, I know there are many who claim to do good but fail in using money contributed for the reasons intended. Do your due diligence in this respect. You don't want your gift to be wasted.

But giving in this way does not excuse you from loving your neighbor in a hands-on manner as well. Love is all that exists in the mind of Christ, so that no matter the situation, we are required to show love, mercy and compassion. There is no other way. Performing these acts of love toward those unable to move forward, which means sometimes merely existing until the next day, will provide a base, or foundation for your mission. Each act of love performed by owning the mind of Christ is one that has the possibility of affecting a positive change in someone's life. That is the power of love. And it is that love to which we must dedicate our lives as children of God.

The devil is a liar

These acts are foundational. They support our other mission of making disciples. We can see this easily because who would want to follow someone who never offered them true love? But the love of God is one that draws us because love is the essence of kindness that overcomes all darkness by fellowship with the creator. The enemy offers companionship but it is no more than a friendship with evil and darkness. And although it may feel good for a long time in our physical bodies, it will always end in destruction, pain and suffering in our spirit. He is a liar. Jesus called him the father of lies. So why would you believe him? His actions are the exact opposite of love. There is no love in him at all. He only seeks your destruction. But the acts of love that are built from employing the mind of Christ will defeat and destroy all the actions of our common enemy because light is more powerful than darkness. We can overcome sin with love.

Seeking God's will for your life

As Christians, the most important thing we can do is to be bathed in, living in, immersed in the will of God. If we are acting outside His will, then we are acting in sin because we are in disobedience to Him. That's something to think about, but something we cannot ignore if we are to maintain a good relationship with God and grow in our Christian walk. I am convinced that if we desire to be close to God, then we must seek His will before we do things that may not be in His will. Submission to

His will is all important to anyone who truly desires to grow in grace and knowledge of Jesus Christ.

> *Romans 12:2*
> *And do not be conformed to this world, but be transformed by the renewing of your mind, that you may **prove** what is that good and acceptable and perfect will of God."*

Good, acceptable, and perfect, each one is a step we must reach before going to the next, and each one is something we must invest in, and make to grow before being given the next. The word *"prove"* in Romans 12:2 means to give evidence. If we claim that we have God's will and that we are performing God's will, there will be evidence that what we are doing *is* God's will. And that evidence will be that what we are doing is "good". So it is only when we make the *"good"* will of God believable in our lives that we are then able to go on to attain the *"acceptable"* will of God. Now, good in this context means exactly that. Good is the opposite of bad and although something may not be bad, it may not be entirely good either. We must accept the fact that in the context given, when concerning the will of God, something referred to as "good" would be something that reflects His holiness and purity and love. To believe otherwise would be denying the "goodness" of God.

The word "acceptable" in this verse is really a unique word. It is the Greek word "euarestos" and it is a compound word that means "good" (eu) and "a very good fit". (arestos) So we can see the correlation between the first "good' and the next step, a good fit. God desires that we have in our lives His good will and that it be something that is right or a good fit for our lives.

God made us unique

It is not God's desire that He destroy our uniqueness when we come to Him. He gave each of us particular talents and gifts and personalities and He in no way desires that we lose those talents and gifts when we come to Him, He only desires that we would use them for His glory, which is only right, because He is worthy, and He is worthy, if for no other reason than that He is willing to forgive us because of the sacrifice of Jesus and grant us eternal life.

The gifts He gives us are what make us unique, so the things He wills us to do, will be those things that fit perfectly with our unique talents and gifts, in other words, a good fit for each of us. For example, if God has given you an outgoing personality and a gift of communication, it is highly unlikely that His will for you would be to join a group of cloistered monks or nuns who must take a vow of silence. It just wouldn't be a good fit.

If God has blessed you with the talent of organization it is likely that His will for you is to be doing something that would utilize your talents. There are many things that could utilize those particular talents, but He probably wouldn't have you doing something for which you are not suited if you are an organized person, such as being a mush stirrer. Monotonously stirring mush does not take much organization. God's plan is that it would be a good fit for the talents with which He has blessed you.

It is only when we make the *"acceptable"* will of God believable in our lives that we are then able to go on to attain the *"perfect"* will of God, one level leading to the next, each level making the next attainable. The word *"perfect"* in Romans 12:2 means complete or of full age, implying spiritual maturity. And those who are spiritually mature live their lives according to the presence of Christ in their lives. In other words, Christ lives through them, they live through Christ, and their lives bear witness of this process. They overcome temptations and are not given to the things of the world. And it is only through this reciprocation that God's perfect or completed will can be accomplished in our lives.

We must learn to reciprocate

Reciprocation means He gave to us in total; now, we give to Him in total. You must see that Jesus giving His life so you would not suffer is Him giving in total. And when we are able to reach the *level of maturity* that brings us to a place of giving to God in total, we can complete the process of transforming by renewal. The word transformed, as described in Romans 12:2, means to change from one state of being to another. It is the Greek word metamorphoo from which we get the word metamorphosis.

And the word renewing, means renovation: taking something old and making it new. Just like if you were to renovate or remodel a room—same space, new room. We can also renovate our minds—still the same person, but a new mind or way of thinking. So transforming is the different stages of change that occur as we renovate the old mind to make it new. Or to put it in Christian terms, transforming is the different stages of growth in God that take us from the carnal or fleshly to the spiritual. And such transformation is only possible in those who come to take on a whole *new way of thinking* as a result of no longer conforming to this world but seeking the will of God. This is one of those things that is easily said, but take a takes a sustained, conscious effort, a lot of work and diligent perseverance to accomplish. Seeking the will of God and discovering the will of God are a cake walk, compared to actually carrying out the will of God, for the very first thing that must be accomplished is that we remove ourselves from sin. Again, sounds easy, but it is a battle, a battle our flesh fights with great enthusiasm.

The path of spiritual transformation that changes our lives is completely contingent upon the renewing of our minds, for it is only through the renewing of our minds that our lives have the ability to change. You see, the mind is like the rudder of a boat—wherever it goes so does the whole boat. So is the mind the rudder of the body that gives direction to our lives. Therefore, it is only through the renewing of our minds that we can direct our lives toward the spiritual transformation that proves what is the *good, acceptable, and perfect* will of God is in each of our lives.

The key to the whole process is transformation. The way we transform is to renew our minds. The way we renew our minds is to stop the old processes, old thinking, old ways of acting out, old ideas that keep coming back and attempt to capture our minds again and again. This is prompted by the Holy Spirit and carried out in our minds.

Destruction of the old man is necessary

If we are to prove God's will in our life, then we must change by destroying the old ways and allowing the new to be built. And it is only when we begin to tear down the old that we take our first step toward investing in the new. This is when we begin to do the *"good"* will of God.

And it is those who continue to tear down the old in order to invest in the new who journey further down the road of self renovation until they have transformed their lives to do the *"acceptable"* will of God. However, those who continue to invest until they have invested it all are the ones who have come to the *"perfect"* or mature will of God by completely tearing down those strongholds that would lead them to a place of self fulfillment and gratification and concentrate on ways they can fulfill God's will by loving Him and loving their neighbor.

There are certain promises that accompany the doing of God's will, both in the Old and New Testaments.

> *Deut 5:29*
> *29 'Oh, that they had such a heart in them that they would fear Me and always keep all My commandments, that it might be well with them and with their children forever!*

> *I Jn 2:16-17*
> *16 For all that is in the world-- the lust of the flesh, the lust of the eyes, and the pride of life-- is not of the Father but is of the world.*
> *17 And the world is passing away, and the lust of it; but he who does the will of God abides forever.*

The will of God is not an elusive thing, but it is only found with some searching and some waiting. When we attempt to discover it, we must be quite certain that we do not impose our own will for our lives in its place. It is so very easy to do.

God's will is not that tough to discover

Some of the ways in which we can discover God's will are right in front of us, and we never even attempt to seek them out. And the reason we don't may be because we know that it will go against the very thing we are contemplating and we don't want to be told what to do.

For example, I know that when we are young and in love, and begin to get very close to someone of the opposite sex, the last thing we want to hear is something like this:

> *1 Thes 4:3-7*
> *3 For this is the will of God, your sanctification: that you should abstain from sexual immorality;*
> *4 that each of you should know how to possess his own vessel in sanctification and honor,*
> *5 not in passion of lust, like the Gentiles who do not know God;*
> *6 that no one should take advantage of and defraud his brother in this matter, because the Lord is the avenger of all such, as we also forewarned you and testified.*
> *7 For God did not call us to uncleanness, but in holiness.*

These are words that may shake our will. They might confuse our plan. They may make us find someplace that doesn't say we need to be in God's will, which will not be found in God's word. Look at the next verse.

> *1 Thes 4:8*
> *8 Therefore he who rejects this does not reject man, but God, who has also given us His Holy Spirit.*

We do not want to reject God, so we will consider his will for our lives. This is one example of seeking God's will in His word. In fact, this book of Thessalonians gives us much good advice about God's will, as do all the New Testament writings. This is why the bible is a very good place to begin seeking God's direction or will for your life. But if you should read it and ignore its advice, you might as well not read it.

God desires to give you a very special place in His kingdom. And He desires to give you a very special job here on earth. He has something very unique and that is made just for you, but we must begin to destroy the old building so that He may help us to construct the new. When we attempt to construct the new on top of the old, both will collapse and we will be in very bad shape indeed. We must look very intensely at our life and decide what needs to be changed, before seeking His will for our life.

Unused knowledge is useless knowledge

Having this knowledge is important. Having the knowledge that we must remodel our lives is very important. But if nothing happens, then it is pretty useless knowledge. If you spend some time drawing up plans to remodel your home, you make them and then remake them and think carefully about those things you desire for your living space, you go down and purchase the lumber and supplies, you put it in neat little piles near where you plan to remodel, but you never actually do any work, then all is for nothing.

It is no different when we seek God's will, His plan for our renovation. If you pray and pray and pray some more, looking deep inside yourself, discovering some faults, some difficulties that most certainly get in the way of your walk with God, but you never really do anything to accomplish the change needed so you can discover the "good" will of God for your life, then you have wasted a lot of time for nothing.

> *Heb 4:1-2*
> *1 Therefore, since the promise of entering his rest still stands, let us be careful that none of you be found to have fallen short of it.*
> *2 For we also have had the gospel preached to us, just as they did; but the message they heard was of no value to them, because those who heard did not combine it with faith.*

Faith is Hebrews 11:1. It speaks of substance and evidence. The first evidence you are seeking God and His will for you is that you no longer seek those things of the world or the flesh. You are now seeking the things of the Spirit so you are able to show love to God and your neighbor. As that happens, you will be seeking the *good* will of God, with that accomplished, you will go on to find the *acceptable* will of God which is that perfect fit for *your* life and ***that*** accomplished, the *perfect* or mature will of God will show up in your life. Each step can only be accomplished by action on the previous step. Each step will bring you to a new place with God.

So I ask you, what is God's will for ***your*** life? Do you see yourself as a missionary, a servant, a teacher, someone who serves through a small ministry to only one or two people? All of these are good and acceptable and perfect in the eyes of God. But you do not need to be any of the above to serve God. Just encounters with those whom God places before you are opportunities to serve and tell others about the love of Christ.

All believers are in ministry

Just know this, God chooses to use every one of His people to minister to some others. It may be in small ways or it may be in not so small ways. Just know that God desires to use the talents and gifts He has given you for His glory and for the edification of His church as well as showing love to your neighbor. Don't let your life be wasted and your gifts be used only for your own edification. Everyone has some time he or she can give back to God, and some*thing* he can give back to God.

What is your gift? What is your talent? Are you using your uniqueness to the glory of God? Are you being all you can be? Look inside yourself and discover what is keeping you from the next level of knowledge of God, so that you can begin to move to the next level. Don't waste another moment, begin today to examine your place on that walk and begin today to move on down the road. As you do, you will discover a new joy that will bring you to your knees before the throne of God as you contemplate His perfect word.

Discipleship is everything

I feel the need to reiterate the importance of being a disciple. It is imperative that we understand this. When Jesus said that if we want to be his disciple, we must pick up our cross and follow Him, He meant it. Following Him is, or should be our main objective. It is the only way we will be able to overcome any sin, from A to Z. I encourage you to read often the gospels which give a complete picture of the mind of Christ. Adopt that vision as your own and begin to make that vision your life. Learn what it means to love God with all your heart, mind and strength and love your neighbor as yourself.

158

Living a life of love is how we overcome sin in our lives. We turn from sin the moment temptation shows up because there is no love in sin. Sin never loves just as love never sins. You can't sin against God if you truly love Him and you won't be able to sin against your neighbor either if you love them. The problem is that we have less than perfect love for either God or our neighbor. Perfect love is agape love. It doesn't need, it provides.

Perfect love gives comfort, aid and direction to those who have none of these. It never becomes angry or impatient but always serves with great joy, for this love comes from the heart of Jesus. If we are disciples of Jesus we will be so filled with this perfect love that sin will be out of the question for us. This is our goal. It is an achievable goal, but it is not an easy goal to reach. This is because sin and temptation are everywhere in this world. We must be aware of our enemy and his actions so we can defend ourselves when it is necessary and pray for them consistently. This is how we defeat our enemies. This is how we will defeat sin. Stay aware of your environment and stay in Christ. You will overcome this way.

Every single action of love we show to those we encounter along the way is a spiritual attack on our enemy. As we love God with all our heart by showing Him honor, praying often, singing praises to Him, keeping joy in our heart and goodness in our minds, and by loving our neighbor each and every day by showing love to those who need to feel love and assisting those in need, we will keep our minds focused on the love of Christ and overcome each and every temptation that is placed before us simply because we are living in the mind of Christ. And that same mind will enable you to go and sin no more and thoroughly enjoy your new life in Christ.

Other books by
David Ross Sherman . .

Available wherever fine books are sold.

Explore the world of joy in Christ. Agalliao is a Greek word that appears eleven times in the New Testament. It means to Jump for joy like a child, but it shows up where it might surprise you

Come experience the love found in the creatures of God. The story of Jenny will make you both laugh and cry as David explores the traits of this amazing animal compared to the One we follow, Jesus

This is the true story of a miracle of which David was party to. It happened in 1983 in Arizona.

Printed in the USA
CPSIA information can be obtained
at www.ICGtesting.com
CBHW021259030724
11005CB00008B/197